W9-CFB-504

rry roasted

cued pizza

nplings pie

les burgers

soup satay

rittata fried

the
chicken
book

Published by Fog City Press
814 Montgomery Street
San Francisco, CA 94133 USA

Copyright © 2002 Weldon Owen Pty Ltd
Reprinted 2002 (three times)

Chief Executive Officer: John Owen
President: Terry Newell
Publisher: Lynn Humphries
Managing Editor: Janine Flew
Art Director: Kylie Mulquin
Editorial Coordinator: Tracey Gibson
Production Manager: Martha Malic-Chavez
Business Manager: Emily Jahn
Vice President International Sales: Stuart Laurence

Project Editor: Margaret Whiskin
Project Designer: Jacqueline Richards
Food Photography: Valerie Martin
Food Stylist: Sally Parker
Home Economist: Christine Sheppard

All rights reserved. Unauthorized reproduction, in any manner, is prohibited.
A catalog record for this book is available from the Library of Congress, Washington, DC.

ISBN 1 876778 82 2

Color reproduction by SC (Sang Choy) International Pte Ltd
Manufactured by Kyodo Printing Co. (S'pore) Pte Ltd
Printed in Singapore

A Weldon Owen Production

the
chicken
book

FOG CITY PRESS

contents

cooking with
chicken

Chicken is so versatile that almost every part can be used in cooking, as the many delicious recipes in this book demonstrate. Chicken is becoming increasingly popular as an economical, relatively low-fat source of protein and an alternative to red meat. For the best results, learn all about chicken—how to choose the correct chicken cut or the best-quality chicken, how to cut up a whole chicken, and how to skin, bone, and store chicken. There is also a recipe for classic chicken stock, including instructions on how to strain the stock, remove the fat, and freeze the stock to keep for other occasions.

The recipes in *The Chicken Book* are divided into the various cooking methods: roasting and baking, frying and sautéing, stir-frying, microwaving, grilling and broiling, and braising, stewing, and casseroling. Each chapter begins with an introductory section that covers the basics of the featured cooking method. These sections include everything you need to know to have each and every recipe turn out beautifully. Included are guidelines on the tools you will need and how to use them, useful tips, and instructions covering basic techniques. For example, you will learn how to prepare a chicken for roasting, how to test for doneness, and how to season, cook, and carve the perfect roast chicken. You will also learn how to pound chicken to a thin, quick-cooking oval, how to marinate chicken pieces, and how to butterfly a whole chicken. If it's frying you want to do, then you will learn the basics of pan frying, sautéing, and stir-frying, including how to chop and bias-slice vegetables for a stir-fry. Or, learn the basics of braising and stewing and how to make your own croutons. If you have a microwave, you'll find hints on how to arrange and rearrange your food in the microwave to ensure quick, even cooking. There is also a glossary that describes how to choose, use, and store many of the ingredients used in the recipes.

The Chicken Book has a variety of recipes from all over the world. You will find traditional recipes for baked chicken, along with classic French, Italian, and Spanish dishes, and Asian and Middle Eastern recipes. Here are some examples to whet your appetite: hearty chicken casserole, Cornish hens with roasted vegetables, oregano and lemon chicken, crispy fried chicken, paella, and chicken pâté. Whether you want a light salad, a sandwich, a burger, or any other kind of chicken dish, you're sure to find something to tempt you among these pages.

With the detailed instructions given in each recipe, both experienced cooks and relative novices can be confident of producing wonderful results every time. There are also handy variations to give you inspirational ideas and to add to your repertoire of delicious, easy-to-make, and impressive recipes.

So, happy cooking!

part One

the basics

all about chicken

Today's chicken has come a long way from its beginnings as a wild fowl in Southeast Asia. Experts believe that chickens were probably domesticated from prehistoric times—there are records that point to chicken-raising in China as early as 1400 BC. During the sixteenth century, chickens were used on board explorers' ships as live food, and so they spread all over the world. But it was not until the twentieth century that the poultry industry was created and chickens became a produce of farms. And it was only during the 1950s that chicken became available to many. Before that it was expensive and available only to the rich and to those who produced it. Today, there are millions of chickens bred each year for eggs and meat, and poultry is a multi-million dollar industry.

Chicken's popularity is well earned. A perfectly roasted chicken, crisp and golden on the outside and moist and succulent on the inside, is hard to beat for good, wholesome home cooking. While roast chicken may be good, it is only one way to cook a chicken. Chicken is so versatile it can be cooked in any way you like. Because it is such a wonderful carrier of other flavors, it lends itself to a wealth of dishes from many different cuisines—everything from traditional roasts to recipes containing rich French herbs and cream, or those with exotic spices from India and Southeast Asia or the pungent combinations from Africa, Mexico, and the Caribbean.

types of chicken

broiler-fryer The most common and least expensive chickens for everyday use are broiler-fryers. These chickens are mass-produced purely for their meat and weigh about 4 lb (2 kg). As the name suggests, they are best broiled (grilled) or fried.

roasting chickens These chickens tend to weigh more than broiler-fryers and can be up to 8 months old. They have a higher fat content and therefore are less likely to dry out with roasting.

free-range chickens The industry regulations that enable poultry farmers to classify their chickens as "free range" vary from place to place. But, generally speaking, the birds must have daytime access to open areas for about half of their life. There are also fewer chickens per meter when they are indoors, and they have to be fed a vegetarian diet that is also free from antibiotics and hormones. There are also different levels of "free range," which also vary from place to place. The birds' living conditions and diet both tend to produce a meatier, slightly larger, and definitely tastier chicken. However, because these chickens are not intensively farmed, they are more expensive than the mass-produced broiler-fryers.

poussins (spatchcock) and Cornish hens
These tiny chickens are very young (about 3 weeks) when they are killed. They are so small that one bird will often only serve one person. The meat is very tender and tasty.

stewing chickens (boilers or fowls)
These chickens are usually larger, older, and tougher than broiler-fryers and so are good for stewing, braising, or making stock.

preparing chicken

Prepackaged, ready-to-cook chicken pieces are widely available and very convenient. However, prepackaged pieces are usually more expensive than a whole chicken of equivalent weight. Also, it is surprisingly simple to cut up a whole chicken yourself—and you know exactly what you are getting. Not only is it easy to cut up a chicken, but it is also simple to skin and bone the pieces to just how you like them. In this section we cover cutting up a whole chicken and skinning and boning chicken pieces.

cutting up a whole chicken

basic tools Another name for cutting up a whole chicken is "jointing." It is called this because you actually cut through the tendons and cartilage of a joint, not through the bone. Because you are not cutting through bone, you don't need special equipment. The two main tools required are a boning knife and poultry shears or kitchen scissors. Boning knives are about 10 inches (25 cm) long and have thin, tapered, flexible blades to allow you to cut around the curves and indentations of meat and bone. Make sure the knife is sharp before doing anything else—a sharp knife is less likely to slip and cut you. Poultry shears have some added spring-lever power but, generally, kitchen scissors will work just as well. Cut up the chicken on a washable acrylic or wooden cutting board—and make sure you wash your hands and every piece of equipment with hot soapy water after handling raw poultry.

1 cutting off the legs Pull one leg away from the body and slit the skin between the thigh and body. Bend back the leg until the thigh bone pops out of the hip joint. With the tip of the knife, cut through the broken joint, meat, and skin to sever the leg. Hold the knife against the backbone as you cut. Repeat with the other leg.

2 separate the legs Place the leg skin-side up. To find the joint, squeeze together the drumstick and thigh—the flat light-colored area at the top is the joint. Cut through the joint to separate the drumstick and thigh into two pieces. Repeat with the other leg.

3 removing the wings Pull one wing away from the body and slit the skin between the wing and the body. Bend back the wing until the joint pops out. Cut through the broken joint, meat, and skin to sever the wing. Repeat with the other wing.

4 separating the breast from the body Using poultry shears, kitchen scissors, or a boning knife, sever the ribs between the breast and back. Cut from the cavity end toward the neck end on both sides. Bend the breast and back halves apart, exposing the joints at the neck that connect the two halves. Cut through the joints.

5 removing the breastbone With the breastbone facing you, using a small knife, slit open the membrane over the breast-bone. Hold the breast at the top and bottom and flex it up—the breastbone will pop out. Pull out the bone with your hand.

6 cutting the breast in half Place the breast skin-side down. Using a boning knife, cut down the center along the groove left by the breastbone. You now have two breast halves.

skinning and boning chicken

Boneless chicken cooks more quickly than pieces with the bone in, and skinning chicken enables you to directly brown the meat. It is also a good idea to score skinless chicken before marinating—this allows the marinade to penetrate the meat. Using these simple techniques, you can prepare the chicken pieces for every cooking method in this book: roasting and baking, frying and sautéing, microwaving, grilling and broiling, stir-frying, braising, stewing, and casseroling, and poaching and boiling.

basic tools The tools for skinning and boning are the same as for cutting up a whole chicken, except you won't need poultry shears (kitchen scissors will certainly do) and you may need a small paring knife (short bladed and pointed), for smaller pieces such as thighs. For skinning, you need hardly any tools—it is mostly done with your hands, with the occasional assistance of a sharp knife or kitchen scissors to cut the skin from the meat.

skinning breasts and thighs Place one breast half, skin-side up, on a cutting board. Holding the half breast with one hand, pull the skin away from the meat with the other, starting at the narrow end. Use the same technique for thighs. As raw chicken tends to be slippery, you may get a better grip if you use a paper towel to hold the pieces.

boning chicken breasts Starting at one side of the ribs, cut the meat away from the bones with a boning knife. Continue cutting, pressing the flat side of the knife blade almost flat against the rib bones. Cut as close to the bone as possible.

removing tendon from the breast

To remove the tendon from the breast, pull it back with your fingers to stretch it out. With a sharp knife, gently scrape the meat away from the tendon until the entire length of the tendon is completely exposed. Sever the tendon and discard.

boning chicken thighs Place the thigh on the cutting board with the meatier side down. With a boning knife or small, sharp knife, make a lengthwise slit through the meat to the bone. Carefully separate the meat from the bone by scraping it away around the bone and at the ends.

Skinning drumsticks or legs With a pair of sharp kitchen scissors, slit the skin from the joint end to the foot end on the shortest side of the drumstick. Remove the skin by holding onto the meaty end and pulling toward the foot end.

carving clues

Despite the mystery surrounding carving chicken, it is really very simple if you use the correct tools and know where and when to cut.

The first thing to remember is to allow the chicken to stand for 15 minutes before carving. This allows the juices to settle so that they don't run out when you carve, and ensures meat that is moist and plump, not dry and stringy.

Place the chicken on a carving board that has a well for catching the juices. Transfer the stuffing to a separate bowl before carving. Use a knife with a long, flexible blade that will maintain a very sharp edge—if the blade is dull, you will ruin even the best-prepared chicken. Also, use a carving fork—a sturdy, oversized fork—to steady the chicken as you carve.

(See page 22 for detailed instructions.)

storing chicken

Careful handling of raw poultry helps prevent the transmission of disease. Chicken must be properly stored in the refrigerator or freezer until it is needed to ensure that it is safe to eat. Leftover cooked chicken and accompaniments such as stuffing should never be allowed to stand at room temperature for more than 2 hours. Before cooking or freezing chicken, rinse it under cold water, let any excess water run off, and pat dry with paper towels.

in the refrigerator

Store fresh chicken in the coldest part of the refrigerator (not above 40°F/2°C). Raw chicken stored in the refrigerator should be used within 2 days, cooked chicken within 2–3 days. To keep stuffing, after the meal, remove all the stuffing from the chicken, along with any remaining meat, and store them in separate containers. Never freeze or refrigerate stuffing in the chicken.

in the freezer

Frozen food keeps best at a temperature of 0°F (minus 18°C). (Check the temperature of your freezer with a freezer thermometer if you are unsure.) You can freeze a whole chicken for up to 1 year, or chicken pieces for up to 6 months. To avoid rough, dry areas on the chicken (where the meat has deteriorated due to exposure to air), freeze chicken airtight and use it within the recommended time.

Sturdy freezer bags and ties are very handy, and are available at most supermarkets. Another option is to use reusable freezer-safe plastic containers. Whatever you choose, always date and note the contents of the container.

The safest and best way to thaw frozen chicken is in the refrigerator. Allow 5 hours of thawing time per 1 lb (500 g). Never defrost chicken at room temperature.

chicken stock

3½ lb (1.75 kg) bony
chicken pieces

3 stalks celery with leaves,
chopped

2 carrots, chopped

1 large onion, chopped

2 sprigs flatleaf (Italian) parsley

½ teaspoon dried thyme, sage,
or basil, crushed

2 bay leaves

salt and pepper to taste

1½ qt (1.5 l) water

◈ In a large saucepan, place the chicken pieces, celery, carrots, onion, parsley, thyme, sage, or basil, bay leaves, and salt and pepper. Add the water. Turn on heat to medium-high and bring to a boil. Reduce heat to low, cover, and simmer for 2 hours. Remove the chicken.

◈ To strain, pour the stock through a large sieve or colander lined with 2 layers of pure cotton cheesecloth (muslin). Discard the vegetables and bay leaves. If using the stock while hot, skim off the fat. (Or, chill the stock and lift off the fat before using.)

◈ If desired, when the bones are cool enough to handle, remove the meat and reserve it for another use. Discard the bones. Store the stock and reserved meat, if any, in separate covered containers in the refrigerator for up to 3 days, or in the freezer for up to 6 months.

part
Two

recipes

roasting and baking
frying and sautéing
stir-frying ❖ microwaving
grilling and broiling
braising, stewing, and casseroling
boiling, steaming, and poaching

roasting *and* baking

roasting and baking basics

To "bake" simply means to cook in an oven—"roast" is to oven-cook in an uncovered pan, usually with frequent basting. With the correct tools and by following a few simple steps, roasting or baking can be the easiest and most satisfying way in which to cook chicken.

Roasting chickens have a high fat content and therefore are the most flavorful, but broiler-fryers also make very good roast chickens. Also, because the smaller poussins (spatchcock) and Cornish game hens have a low meat-to-bone ratio, they are tender and full of flavor.

The first thing you need for successful roasting and baking is an oven thermometer. Some of the most common problems with roasting and baking occur because the oven is too hot, or not hot enough. With chicken, it is vital that you do not undercook; undercooked chicken may harbor dangerous salmonella bacteria. And it is very easy to overcook chicken and rob it of all its wonderful juices. Oven thermostats are rarely accurate and an oven thermometer will give you an accurate reading. You will be amazed at what this simple instrument will do for your confidence—it makes your results much more predictable.

For roasting, it is essential to have a roasting pan. A roasting pan has a roasting rack, which raises the chicken above the pan and the juices. This allows for even cooking and browning and prevents the chicken from sitting in the juices or sticking to the pan.

roasting and baking basics

A brush or bulb baster, for basting chicken, is essential for good results. Basting adds flavor and stops the chicken from drying out. Other handy items are common household string (for tying chicken) and kitchen scissors (for trimming it of excess fat).

To test a whole chicken for doneness, grasp the end of a drumstick—if it easily moves up and down and twists in its socket, it is done. To test other cuts, skewer the chicken meat in the thickest part; when the juices run clear, it is done. Another way is to use a meat thermometer. Insert an instant-read thermometer into the center of the inside thigh muscle, being careful not to touch bone—the temperature should be 180°F (82°C).

To carve a whole chicken, remove it from the oven when it is done, cover with aluminum foil, and let it stand for 15 minutes. This allows the juices that are drawn to the surface to recirculate and firm up the chicken. Otherwise, when you carve, the juices will run out and the chicken will be dry and will shred. Before you begin, make sure you have a sharp carving knife and a two-pronged fork (to hold the chicken steady). First, cut the legs from the chicken: Simply pull each leg away and cut through the skin between the thigh and the body. With skin-side up, cut through the joint between the drumstick and the thigh. Remove the breast meat by cutting along one side of the breastbone and down the rib bones. Then slice the breast meat. Finally, remove the wings by cutting through the joints where the wing bones and backbone meet.

To stuff a chicken, put the stuffing in the neck cavity, pull the skin over the opening, and secure it with a metal skewer. Stuff the body cavity and tie the drumsticks together with string to cover the cavity. Do not stuff the cavities full because stuffing usually expands with cooking.

basic roast chicken

serves 6

1 whole chicken,
3–3½ lb (1.5–1.8 kg)

vegetable oil or melted
margarine or butter

1½ tablespoons mixed dried
herbs, such as sage, thyme,
oregano, and/or rosemary

❖ Preheat oven to 375°F (190°C/Gas Mark 4).

❖ Tie the chicken legs to tail, skewer neck skin to back, and twist the wings under the back. Brush the bird with oil, margarine, or butter and sprinkle with herbs. Place the chicken, breast-side up, on a rack in a roasting pan. Place in oven and roast until cooked through, 1¼–1½ hours, basting with pan juices occasionally. Cover loosely with aluminum foil and let stand in a warm place for 15 minutes before carving.

chicken and pumpkin
diamonds
with herbed cream

serves 6

3 cups (24 oz/750 g) cooked mashed pumpkin, cooled

1 lb (500 g) cooked chicken meat, finely chopped

½ cup (4 oz/125 g) butter, melted

1 cup (6 oz/180 g) semolina flour

½ cup (4½ oz/140 g) ricotta cheese

½ cup (1¾ oz/50 g) grated Parmesan cheese

6 green (spring) onions, chopped

2 cloves garlic, crushed

5 eggs, lightly beaten

salt and pepper to taste

HERBED CREAM SAUCE

2 teaspoons olive oil

4 cloves garlic, crushed

½ cup (4 fl oz/125 ml) dry white wine

½ cup (4 fl oz/125 ml) chicken stock

1 cup (8 fl oz/250 ml) heavy (double) cream

2 tablespoons chopped fresh basil

2 tablespoons chopped fresh oregano

2 tablespoons chopped fresh chives

salt and white pepper to taste

✤ Preheat oven to 400°F (200°C/Gas Mark 5). Lightly grease a 3- x 9-inch (30- x 25-cm) baking dish.

✤ In a large bowl, combine the pumpkin, chicken, butter, flour, cheeses, green onion, garlic, eggs, and salt and pepper. Mix well. Spread the mixture evenly into the prepared dish and smooth over the top. Bake until firm, about 40 minutes.

✤ For the sauce, in a small saucepan over medium heat, warm the oil. Add the garlic and cook, stirring, until lightly browned, about 5 minutes. Add the wine and stock and simmer, uncovered, until reduced to about ½ cup (4 fl oz/125 ml), about 5 minutes. Add the cream and herbs and stir until hot. Add salt and pepper.

✤ Cut the baked chicken and pumpkin mixture into small diamond shapes, divide them between warmed serving dishes, and spoon over the sauce. Serve hot.

storage hint

This recipe can be made a day ahead and kept covered, separately, in the refrigerator.

. . . .

The baked pumpkin and chicken mixture is suitable for freezing.

chicken pizza
with mushrooms and artichokes

serves 4–6

2 green bell peppers (capsicums), quartered

2 tablespoons olive oil

2 onions, sliced

2 cloves garlic, crushed

10 oz (300 g) oyster mushrooms, halved

2 x 15-oz (430-g) prepared pizza bases

1/3 cup (3 fl oz/90 ml) tomato paste

1 tablespoon extra-virgin olive oil

2 tablespoons chopped fresh basil

1 lb (500 g) mozzarella cheese, shredded

1 lb (500 g) cooked chicken meat, sliced

2 x 6-oz (170-g) jars marinated artichoke hearts, drained

1/3 cup (1 oz/30 g) drained, oil-packed, sun-dried tomatoes, sliced

1/3 cup (2 1/2 oz/75 g) drained black Riviera olives (see note on page 27)

ground black pepper to taste

Preheat oven to 500°F (250°C/Gas Mark 7). Turn on broiler (griller).

Broil (grill) the bell peppers, skin-side up, 4–5 inches (10–12 cm) from heat, until skin blisters and blackens, about 10 minutes. Place hot bell peppers in a plastic bag, seal, and leave for 10 minutes or until cool enough to handle. (The steam created will make the peppers easier to peel.) Peel and slice thinly.

In a frying pan over medium heat, combine the 2 tablespoons olive oil, onions, garlic, and mushrooms. Cook, stirring, until onions are soft, about 5 minutes.

Place the pizza bases on baking sheets. Combine the tomato paste, extra-virgin olive oil, and basil and spread on the pizza bases. Top with half the cheese then the chicken, artichokes, mushroom mixture, bell peppers, tomatoes, olives, and remaining cheese. Sprinkle with ground black pepper and bake until browned and hot, about 15 minutes. Using a pizza cutter or sharp knife, cut into wedges. Serve hot.

recipe **hint**

Riviera olives are tiny black olives bottled in brine— substitute larger olives if Riviera are unavailable.

This recipe can be prepared a day ahead—assemble just before baking.

italian chicken with pesto mayonnaise

PESTO MAYONNAISE

2 red bell peppers (capsicums), quartered

1 bunch (1¼ lb/625 g) leaf (English) spinach, washed

1½ lb (750 g) skinless, boneless chicken breast halves

5 oz (155 g) thinly sliced mild salami

¼ cup (1 oz/30 g) drained, oil-packed, sun-dried tomatoes, thinly sliced

5 oz (155 g) shredded mozzarella cheese

black pepper to taste

1 tablespoon olive oil

1 clove garlic, crushed

1 cup (1 oz/30 g) lightly packed basil leaves

1 clove garlic, crushed

2 tablespoons grated Parmesan cheese

¼ cup (2 fl oz/60 ml) olive oil

½ cup (4 fl oz/125 ml) bought mayonnaise

salt and pepper to taste

◈ Preheat oven to 375°F (190°C/Gas Mark 4). Turn on broiler (griller).

◈ Broil (grill) the bell peppers, skin-side up, 4–5 inches (10–12 cm) from heat, until skin blisters and blackens, about 10 minutes. Place bell peppers in a plastic bag, seal, and leave for 10 minutes or until cool enough to handle. (The steam created will make the bell peppers easier to peel.) Peel and cut into strips.

◈ Boil, steam, or microwave spinach until just wilted. Drain well and pat dry with paper towels.

◈ Place each chicken breast half between plastic wrap and, using the flat side of a meat mallet, gently pound to even out thickness and square off. Lay the spinach leaves evenly over the chicken, then top with the salami, roasted peppers, tomatoes, and mozzarella cheese. Sprinkle with pepper and press down firmly. Roll up tightly and secure each roll with string at 1-inch (2.5-cm) intervals. Mix together the oil and garlic and brush over the rolls. Bake until cooked through, about 1 hour. Leave to cool, then refrigerate for several hours.

◈ For the mayonnaise, in a blender or food processor, blend or process the basil, garlic, Parmesan cheese, and oil until smooth. In a bowl, combine the basil mixture and mayonnaise and add salt and pepper, mixing well. Keep tightly covered until required.

◈ Remove the string from the chicken and slice thinly. Serve with the pesto mayonnaise.

chicken and basil loaf

serves 6

10 thin slices (rashers) bacon
(about 8 oz/250 g total), rind removed

1 onion, chopped

2 cloves garlic, crushed

1/2 cup (1/2 oz/15 g) chopped fresh basil

1 1/2 lb (750 g) ground (minced) chicken
meat

2 cups (4 oz/125 g) stale bread crumbs

3/4 cup (6 fl oz/190 ml) heavy (double)
cream

1 egg, lightly beaten

1/2 cup (1 3/4 oz/50 g) grated Parmesan
cheese

ground black pepper to taste

ONION-PEPPER RELISH

3 red bell peppers (capsicums)

2 tablespoons butter

10 oz (300 g) small onions,
sliced lengthwise

1/3 cup (2 1/2 oz/75 g) superfine (caster) sugar

1/3 cup (3 fl oz/90 ml) dry red wine

2 tablespoons balsamic vinegar

❖ Preheat oven to 350°F (180°C/Gas Mark 4). Line a 9- x 5-inch (23- x 13-cm) loaf dish with 9 slices of bacon, leaving the ends of the bacon overhanging the edges of the dish.

❖ In a bowl, combine the onion, garlic, basil, chicken, bread crumbs, cream, egg, Parmesan, and pepper. Mix well. Press the mixture firmly into the prepared dish. Fold the overhanging bacon over the mixture and lay the remaining bacon slice along the center. Cover the dish with aluminum foil and place in a baking dish. Add enough boiling water to come halfway up the sides of the loaf dish. Bake until firm, about 1½ hours. Cool slightly, then pour off accumulated liquid from the top of the loaf. Turn out and slice.

❖ For the relish, turn on broiler (griller). Broil (grill) peppers, 4–5 inches (10–12 cm) from heat, until skin blisters and blackens, about 10 minutes. Place hot bell peppers in a plastic bag, seal, and leave for 10 minutes or until cool enough to handle. (The steam created will make the bell peppers easier to peel.) Peel and slice thinly.

❖ In a medium saucepan over low heat, warm the butter. Add the onions and cook, covered, until soft, about 10 minutes. Add the sugar, wine, vinegar, and peppers and simmer, uncovered, until most of the liquid has evaporated, about 15 minutes.

❖ Serve the loaf warm or cold, with the relish.

garlic chicken with goats' cheese bruschetta

serves 6

This recipe is very simple to make and is an interesting twist on the traditional roast chicken recipe. The use of classic Italian herbs and Italian garlic bread, or bruschetta, gives this old favorite freshness and sophistication.

2 sprigs fresh rosemary

2 sprigs fresh thyme

1 whole chicken, about 3¹/₂ lb (1.8 kg)

1 lb (500 g) garlic heads (bulbs)

¹/₄ cup (2 fl oz/60 ml) olive oil

2 tablespoons butter, melted

salt and black pepper to taste

GOATS' CHEESE BRUSCHETTA

1 large baguette (French stick)

¹/₄ cup (2 fl oz/60 ml) olive oil

2 tablespoons olive paste or pâté

2 tablespoons sun-dried tomato paste or pâté

3¹/₂ oz (100 g) goats' cheese, crumbled

1 tablespoon chopped fresh thyme

✧ Preheat oven to 375°F (190°C/Gas Mark 4).

✧ Place rosemary and thyme in the cavities of the chicken. Tie the chicken legs to tail, skewer neck skin to back, and twist the wings under the back. Break the garlic into cloves (do not peel). Place the chicken in a baking dish and put the garlic around the chicken. Combine the oil and butter and brush and/or drizzle the chicken and garlic with the mixture. Sprinkle with salt and pepper. Bake until chicken is cooked through, about 1¾ hours. Stir garlic occasionally.

✧ When the chicken is done, remove from the oven, cover with aluminum foil, and leave to stand in a warm place for 15 minutes.

✧ While the chicken is standing, make the goats' cheese bruschetta. Turn on broiler (griller). Slice the bread diagonally into ½-inch (1.25-cm) thick slices (you will need about 18 slices). Lightly brush both sides of the bread with oil and broil (grill) on one side until lightly browned. Spread half the slices with olive paste and half with sun-dried tomato paste. Sprinkle with the goats' cheese and thyme and broil until lightly browned.

✧ Serve the chicken drizzled with pan juices and accompanied with the warm bruschetta.

chicken and leek pie

serves 6–8

2 cups (8 oz/250 g) all-purpose (plain) flour

5 oz (155 g) cream cheese, chopped

⅓ cup (3 oz/90 g) butter, chopped

3 egg yolks

1 tablespoon water, plus 2 teaspoons extra

FILLING

1 tablespoon vegetable oil

1½ lb (750 g) chicken breast meat, chopped

2 leeks, sliced

3 slices (rashers) bacon, chopped

2 cloves garlic, crushed

3 tablespoons butter

2 tablespoons all-purpose (plain) flour

½ cup (4 fl oz/125 ml) dry white wine

1 cup (8 fl oz/250 ml) milk

⅓ cup (1½ oz/45 g) shredded Cheddar cheese

⅓ cup (1 oz/30 g) grated Parmesan cheese

2 teaspoons grain mustard

1 tablespoon chopped fresh thyme

salt and pepper to taste

❖ Preheat oven to 400°F (200°C/Gas Mark 5). Lightly grease a 10-inch (25-cm) pie dish.

❖ Sift the flour into a bowl. Rub in the cream cheese and butter. Add 2 of the egg yolks and about 1 tablespoon of water. Knead dough until smooth, cover, and refrigerate for 30 minutes.

❖ Divide the dough in half. Roll out one half into a circle large enough to line the bottom and sides of the pie dish; trim edges. Cover pastry with aluminum foil or parchment (baking) paper and fill with dried beans or rice. Bake for 15 minutes. Remove foil or paper and beans and bake until pastry is lightly browned, about 10 minutes more. Remove from oven and leave to cool.

❖ For the filling, in a medium frying pan over medium-high heat, warm the oil. Add the chicken in batches and cook, stirring, until browned, about 4 minutes. Remove the chicken. Add the leeks, bacon, and garlic and cook, stirring, until leeks are soft, about 5 minutes. Add the butter and flour and cook, stirring, until the liquid is bubbling, about 1 minute.

❖ Remove pan from heat and gradually add the wine and milk. Return to heat and cook, stirring, until the mixture boils and thickens. Stir in the cheeses, mustard, thyme, and chicken. Mix well and add salt and pepper. Remove from heat and leave the filling to cool slightly.

❖ Spoon filling into the pastry shell. Combine the remaining egg yolk with the 2 teaspoons extra water and brush the edges of the pastry shell with the mixture. Roll out the second half of dough into a circle large enough to fit the top of the pie. Cover the pie with the dough and press the edges together firmly. Trim, then pinch edges together. Brush pastry with more egg yolk mixture. Cut two slits in the pastry. Bake until golden brown and hot, about 35 minutes.

serves 4

1 tablespoon vegetable oil

4 skinless, boneless chicken breast halves (1 lb/500 g total)

1 tablespoon butter

2¹⁄₂ cups (8 oz/250 g) fresh mushrooms, finely chopped

2 green (spring) onions, finely chopped

1 tablespoon dry white vermouth or dry white wine (optional)

salt and pepper to taste

¹⁄₄ teaspoon dried thyme, crushed

2 tablespoons sour cream

8 sheets filo dough

¹⁄₃ cup (3 oz/90 g) butter, melted

❖ Preheat oven to 375°F (190°C/Gas Mark 4).

❖ In a large frying pan over high heat, warm the oil. Add the chicken breasts and brown on both sides. Remove chicken and set aside.

❖ In the same pan, melt the butter over medium-high heat. Add the mushrooms and green onions and cook, stirring, until most of the liquid evaporates, about 5 minutes. Stir in vermouth or wine (if using), salt and pepper, and thyme. Cook until the liquid evaporates, 2–3 minutes. Cool, then stir in sour cream.

❖ Brush 1 sheet of filo with some of the melted butter. Place another sheet atop the first and brush it with butter. (Keep remaining filo covered with a damp towel.) Place a chicken breast in the center of one narrow end. Spread the chicken with one-fourth of the mushroom mixture. Fold both long sides of filo toward the center and brush with butter. Roll up.

❖ Place the chicken on a baking sheet and brush the top and sides with butter. Repeat with the remaining filo, mushroom mixture, chicken breasts, and butter.

❖ Bake until filo is golden and chicken is cooked through, about 25 minutes. Serve hot.

chicken wrapped in filo

olive-seasoned chicken

serves 4–6

1 whole chicken, about 3½ lb (1.8 kg)

⅓ cup (3 oz/90 g) butter, at room temperature

½ cup (3½ oz/100 g) finely chopped pitted black olives

4 cloves garlic, crushed

ground black pepper to taste

12 baby onions (about 10 oz/ 315 g), peeled

8 oz (250 g) red cherry tomatoes

8 oz (250 g) yellow pear (teardrop) tomatoes

½ cup (½ oz/15 g) lightly packed whole fresh basil leaves

❖ Preheat oven to 400°F (200°C/ Gas Mark 5).

❖ Carefully loosen the skin from the chicken over the breast.

❖ Place butter, olives, and garlic in a bowl and combine with a wooden spoon. Spoon the mixture under the skin of the chicken and, using your hands, ease it evenly over the flesh. Tie the legs together and tuck the wings under the body. Sprinkle with pepper and place in a baking dish. Roast for 45 minutes.

❖ Add the onions, coat them in the pan juices, and roast for 30 minutes. Add the tomatoes and basil and roast until the chicken is cooked through, a further 15 minutes. '

❖ Remove from the oven and let stand for 5 minutes, then remove the string. Serve with the onions, tomatoes, and basil. Drizzle with pan juices, if desired.

chicken and almond salad

serves 6

3 skinless, boneless chicken breast halves (12 oz/375 g total)

salt and pepper to taste

2/3 cup (5 fl oz/155 ml) water

1 Boston or Bibb (mignonette) lettuce, torn into serving pieces

2 cups (2 oz/60 g) lightly packed watercress sprigs

LEMON MAYONNAISE

2 eggs

1/3 cup (3 fl oz/90 ml) lemon juice

2 tablespoons Dijon mustard

1 cup (8 fl oz/250 ml) light olive oil

1/2 cup (4 fl oz/125 ml) peanut oil

grated zest of 2 lemons

1/3 cup (2 oz/60 g) toasted almonds, to serve

2 tablespoons grated lemon zest, to serve

❖ Preheat oven to 300°F (150°C/ Gas Mark 2).

❖ Place the chicken, in a single layer, in a baking dish. Sprinkle with salt and pepper. Add the water and bake until cooked through, 30 minutes. Remove from dish and cut into strips. Combine with salad greens in a large bowl.

❖ For the mayonnaise, place the eggs, lemon juice, and mustard in the bowl of a food processor. Process for 1 minute. Combine the oils and, with the motor running, add oils in a slow, steady stream. Process until thoroughly combined. Stir in the lemon zest.

❖ Toss the mayonnaise with the greens and chicken and sprinkle with the almonds and lemon zest. Serve soon after preparing.

smoked chicken pizza

serves 2–4

PIZZA DOUGH

½ cup (7 oz/220 g) whole wheat (wholemeal) flour

1 tablespoon baking powder

½ teaspoon salt

½ cup (4 fl oz/125 ml) water, plus 2 tablespoons extra as needed

2 tablespoons olive oil

TOPPING

½ cup (4 fl oz/125 g) purchased tomato pasta sauce

8 oz (250 g) smoked chicken, sliced

3½ oz (100 g) goats' cheese, crumbled

❖ Preheat oven to 450°F (230°C/Gas Mark 6). Place a baking sheet in oven.

❖ For the dough, combine the flour, baking powder, and salt. Make a well in the center. Add the ½ cup (4 fl oz/125 ml) water and the oil and gently combine, adding some of the extra water if needed. Transfer to a floured work surface and knead until smooth and elastic, 5–7 minutes. Press out the dough into an 11-inch (28-cm) circle.

❖ Place the dough on the baking sheet. Spoon the tomato sauce over the base, and top it with the smoked chicken then the goats' cheese.

❖ Bake until the pizza is golden on the edges and crisp underneath, about 20 minutes. Serve hot.

chunky
chicken pie

serves 8

CHEDDAR PASTRY

2 cups (10 oz/315 g) all-purpose
(plain) flour

¾ cup (6 oz/185 g) butter, chilled,
cut into small pieces

1 cup (4 oz/125 g) shredded sharp
Cheddar cheese

½ cup (4 fl oz/125 ml) ice water

FILLING

2¼ cups (18 fl oz/560 ml) chicken stock

2 skinless, boneless whole chicken
breasts, about 1½ lb (750 g) total

salt to taste

2½ cups (12 oz/375 g) baby carrots,
cut into 1-inch (2.5-cm) pieces

3 celery stalks, thickly sliced

10 oz (315 g) pearl (baby) onions, peeled

1 cup (5 oz/155 g) loose-pack frozen peas

⅓ cup (3 oz/90 g) unsalted butter

½ cup (2 oz/60 g) all-purpose
(plain) flour

1 cup (8 fl oz/250 ml) heavy
(double) cream

salt and ground black pepper to taste

1 teaspoon minced fresh thyme

3 tablespoons chopped fresh chives

3 tablespoons minced fresh flatleaf
(Italian) parsley

1 egg, lightly beaten

chunky chicken pie

Simple, pastry-topped meat stews originated long ago in England and the humble meat pie has been satisfying appetites around the world ever since. This recipe uses boneless chicken breasts and baby vegetables to create a deliciously filling pie.

❖ To make the pastry, place the flour in a bowl. Using a pastry blender or your fingertips, work in the butter until the mixture is crumbly. Add the cheese and work in until just blended. Sprinkle ice water over the pastry dough, a little at a time, and gather the pastry into a ball. Knead until just combined. Wrap in plastic wrap and chill.

❖ For the filling, in a saucepan over medium heat, bring the stock to a simmer. Add the chicken and simmer, uncovered, until cooked through, 15–20 minutes. Remove from the heat and let the chicken cool completely in the liquid. Remove the chicken breasts and reserve the stock. Cut the chicken into ¾-inch (2-cm) chunks.

❖ Bring a saucepan three-fourths full of lightly salted water to a boil over medium-high heat. Add carrots and cook for 5–6 minutes. Add celery, onions, and peas and cook until tender, 3 minutes. Drain and reserve enough liquid to add to the chicken stock to make 2½ cups (20 fl oz/625 ml).

chunky chicken pie

✥ In a saucepan over medium heat, melt the butter. Sprinkle in the flour and whisk until the mixture is gently bubbling and smooth, 2–3 minutes. Do not brown. Gradually add the reserved stock mixture, whisking constantly, and bring to a simmer. Cook, stirring often, until smooth and slightly thickened, 4–5 minutes. Add the cream and cook, stirring occasionally, until the sauce coats the back of the spoon, about 5 minutes more. Remove from the heat and stir in the salt and pepper, thyme, chives, and parsley.

✥ Preheat oven to 400°F (200°C/Gas Mark 5). Add the chicken and vegetables to the sauce and stir to combine. Spoon into a 9- x 13-inch (23- x 33-cm) baking dish. Brush the edge of the dish with some of the beaten egg.

✥ On a lightly floured surface, roll out the pastry into a 10- x 15-inch (25- x 38-cm) rectangle. Transfer pastry to dish, pressing the edges firmly. Trim away the overhang. Gently knead the dough scraps together. Roll the dough out to about ⅛ inch (3 mm) thick, and cut out several small leaf shapes. Brush the top of the pie with the beaten egg. Using a knife, score the pastry leaves lightly, attach to the top of the pie, and brush with more egg. Cut 3 slits, each 1 inch (2.5 cm) long, at the center of the pie.

✥ Bake until golden, 25–30 minutes. Remove from oven and let stand for 5 minutes, then spoon onto warmed individual plates or bowls. Serve hot.

wild rice chicken
with grand marnier glaze

serves 6

½ cup (3½ oz/100 g) wild rice

1 tablespoon vegetable oil

1 onion, chopped

1 clove garlic, crushed

1 stalk celery, chopped

¼ cup (¾ oz/20 g) chopped fresh chives

½ cup (1 oz/30 g) stale bread crumbs

½ cup (1¾ oz/50 g) chopped pecans

1 egg, lightly beaten

salt and pepper to taste

1 whole chicken, 3–3½ lb (1.5–1.8 kg)

1 tablespoon orange marmalade mixed with
1 tablespoon Grand Marnier liqueur

SAUCE

¾ cup (6 fl oz/180 ml) dry white wine

¼ cup (2 oz/60 g) orange marmalade

1 tablespoon cornstarch (cornflour),
plus 1 teaspoon extra

1 cup (8 fl oz/250 ml) orange juice

2 teaspoons Grand Marnier liqueur

❖ Preheat oven to 400°F (200°C/Gas Mark 5).

❖ For the seasoning, bring a medium saucepan of water to a boil over medium heat. Add the rice and cook, uncovered, until just tender, 20–30 minutes. Drain. In a saucepan over medium heat, warm the oil. Add the onion, garlic, and celery. Cook, stirring, until the onion is soft, about 5 minutes. Remove from heat and cool. In a bowl, combine the rice and onion mixture with the chives, bread crumbs, pecans, egg, and salt and pepper. Mix well.

❖ Stuff the chicken with the seasoning. Tie the chicken legs to tail, skewer neck skin to back, and twist the wings under the back. Place the chicken on a wire rack in a roasting pan and pour ¼ cup (2 fl oz/60 ml) water into the dish. Bake, uncovered, for 1 hour. Brush chicken with the marmalade-Grand Marnier mixture and bake until cooked through, about 30 minutes more.

❖ For the sauce, in a small saucepan over medium heat, combine the wine, marmalade, cornstarch, and ¼ cup (2 fl oz/60 ml) of the orange juice. Stir until the mixture boils and thickens. Stir in the remaining orange juice and the Grand Marnier and keep stirring until hot.

❖ When the chicken is cooked through, cover with aluminum foil and let stand in a warm place for 15 minutes. Remove string before carving. Serve with the sauce.

chicken satay pizza

serves 2–4

With just a few cleverly used ingredients, it's easy to turn a pizza into a gourmet treat. Mozzarella cheese is perfect for pizzas because of its excellent melting qualities and its mild taste that complements just about any other topping.

4 oz (250 g) skinless, boneless chicken breasts

⅓ cup (3 fl oz/90 ml) satay (peanut) sauce

1 tablespoon olive oil

CORNMEAL PIZZA DOUGH

½ cup (2½ oz/75 g) yellow cornmeal (polenta)

4 oz (125 g) all-purpose (plain) flour

2 teaspoons baking powder

½ teaspoon salt

½ cup (4 fl oz/125 ml) water, plus extra as needed

2 tablespoons olive oil

½ cup (⅓ oz/10 g) bean sprouts

½ cup (1¾ oz/50 g) shredded mozzarella cheese

✧ Preheat oven to 450°F (230°C/Gas Mark 6). Place a baking sheet in the oven.

✧ Thinly slice the chicken. Mix 1 tablespoon of the satay sauce with the olive oil. Combine the chicken and sauce mixture and marinate in the refrigerator for at least 20 minutes.

✧ For the pizza dough, in a large bowl, combine the cornmeal, flour, baking powder, and salt. Make a well in the center and add the water and oil. Combine by gradually incorporating the flour into the liquid, adding a little extra water if necessary.

✧ Turn the dough out onto a floured work surface and knead until smooth and elastic, 5–7 minutes. Using your fingertips, press out the dough into a 9-inch (22-cm) circle.

✧ Place the dough on the heated baking sheet. Spread with the remaining satay sauce and then top with the chicken, bean sprouts, and mozzarella.

✧ Bake until the pizza is golden on the edges and crisp underneath, about 15 minutes. Using a pizza cutter or sharp knife, cut the pizza into serving pieces. Serve hot.

barbecued chicken
pan pizza

This recipe has the traditional ingredients of a pizza—tomato sauce and mozzarella cheese—but with a Mexican twist. It's simple to make and very impressive. The tortilla pizza dough has a wonderful fluffy texture and gives this pizza a full and satisfying taste. The combination of chicken, corn, and cheese is always a favorite.

TORTILLA PIZZA DOUGH

½ cup (2 oz/60 g) all-purpose (plain) flour

1 cup (4 oz/125 g) tortilla flour (masa harina), extra-fine cornmeal (polenta), or millet meal

2 teaspoons baking powder

½ teaspoon salt

⅓ cup (2½ fl oz/80 ml) water, plus extra as needed

2 tablespoons olive oil

½ cup (4 fl oz/125 ml) purchased or home-made tomato pasta sauce

8 oz (250 g) barbecued chicken meat, shredded

½ cup (3 oz/100 g) cooked corn kernels

¼ cup (30 g/1 oz) shredded mozzarella cheese

1 tablespoon chopped fresh flatleaf (Italian) parsley

◈ Preheat oven to 450°F (230°C/Gas Mark 6). Place a baking sheet in the oven.

◈ For the pizza dough, in a large bowl, combine the flours, baking powder, and salt. Make a well in the center and add the water and oil. Combine by gradually incorporating the flour into the liquid, adding a little extra water if necessary.

◈ Transfer the dough to a floured work surface and knead until smooth and elastic, 5–7 minutes. Using your fingertips, press out the dough into a 10-inch (25-cm) circle.

◈ Place the dough on the baking sheet. Spread the tomato sauce over the pizza base then top with the chicken, corn, and mozzarella.

◈ Bake until the pizza is golden on the edges and crisp underneath, about 15 minutes. Using a pizza cutter or sharp knife, cut into serving pieces. Serve hot, sprinkled with the parsley.

seasoned
chicken breasts
with creamy sauce

serves 4

4 skinless, boneless chicken breast halves
(1 lb/500 g total)

3 tablespoons butter

2 slices (rashers) bacon, chopped

2 leeks, trimmed and finely chopped

1 clove garlic, crushed

1/3 cup (1 1/2 oz/40 g) drained sun-dried
tomatoes, finely chopped

1/4 cup (1 oz/30 g) grated Parmesan cheese

2 teaspoons grain mustard

2 tablespoons chopped fresh basil,
plus 2 teaspoons extra

1 tablespoon vegetable oil,
plus 2 teaspoons extra

1/2 cup (4 fl oz/125 ml) dry white wine

1/2 cup (4 fl oz/125 ml) chicken stock

1/2 cup (4 fl oz/125 ml) heavy (double)
cream

1 teaspoon cornstarch (cornflour)

1 teaspoon cold water

✧ Preheat oven to 400°F (200°C/Gas Mark 5).

✧ Remove the tenderloins (supremes) from the chicken breasts. Remove the white sinew from the tenderloins. In a food processor, finely grind (mince) the tenderloins.

✧ In a frying pan over medium heat, melt the butter. Add the bacon, leeks, and garlic and cook, stirring, until the leeks are soft, about 8 minutes. Add the sun-dried tomatoes and mix well. Remove from heat and reserve ¼ cup (2 fl oz/60 ml) of the mixture for the sauce. Combine the remaining mixture with the cheese, mustard, 2 tablespoons basil, and the ground chicken. Mix well.

✧ Cut a pocket in one side of each chicken breast, taking care not to cut all the way through. Carefully push one-fourth of the stuffing into each pocket and secure with toothpicks.

✧ In a medium frying pan over medium heat, warm the 1 tablespoon oil. Add the chicken and cook until well browned on both sides, about 5 minutes total. Transfer the chicken to a baking dish and bake until the chicken is cooked through, about 15 minutes.

✧ Meanwhile, heat the extra 2 teaspoons of oil in a small frying pan. Add the reserved bacon mixture and cook until heated through. Add the wine and stock and simmer, uncovered, until the mixture is reduced by half, about 10 minutes. Combine the cream, cornstarch, and water and add to the pan. Stir until the sauce boils and thickens slightly. Stir in the extra basil.

✧ Remove the toothpicks from the chicken. Slice and serve with the sauce.

sausages
with bell peppers

serves 4–6

In small pizzerias, the *forno a legna*, or "wood-fired pizza oven," is often used for preparing simple main courses such as this hearty dish of roasted sausages and bell peppers. This recipe can also be made with traditional Italian sausages, which may be mild or highly spiced and made with or without fennel.

8 chicken sausages (about 1 lb/500 g total)

10 fresh thyme sprigs

2 tablespoons extra-virgin olive oil

1 large red (Spanish) onion, cut in half through the stem end and thinly sliced

3 cloves garlic, minced

4 red bell peppers (capsicums), cut lengthwise into strips ¼ inch (6 mm) wide

¼ cup (⅓ oz/10 g) coarsely chopped fresh flatleaf (Italian) parsley

salt and ground black pepper to taste

◈ Preheat oven to 450°F (230°C/Gas Mark 6).

◈ Arrange the sausages in a single layer in a roasting pan just large enough to hold them. Tuck the thyme around them. Pour in water to a depth of ½ inch (12 mm). Bake, turning the sausages once or twice, until the water has completely evaporated and the sausages are evenly browned, 10–15 minutes.

◈ In a frying pan over medium-low heat, warm the olive oil. Add the onion and cook, stirring occasionally, until soft, 5–6 minutes. Add the garlic and cook for 1 minute more. Stir in the bell peppers and cook, stirring occasionally, until they just begin to soften, about 10 minutes.

◈ To the roasting pan, add the bell pepper mixture, parsley, and salt and pepper. Return the pan to the oven and continue to bake until the sausages are a deep golden brown and the vegetables golden, a further 15 minutes. Transfer to a warmed platter and serve immediately.

cornish hens
with roasted vegetables

serves 4

2 Cornish game hens (spatchcocks),
(3–4 lb/1.5–2 kg total), halved

MARINADE

⅓ cup (3 fl oz/80 ml) extra-virgin olive oil

½ cup (4 fl oz/125 ml) balsamic vinegar

1 tablespoon chopped garlic

3 tablespoons chopped shallots

4 teaspoons fresh rosemary leaves or
2 teaspoons dried rosemary

15 fresh sage leaves or 1 teaspoon ground
dried sage

2 bay leaves

freshly ground black pepper to taste

VEGETABLES

2 large broccoli florets

2 large cauliflower florets

1 zucchini (courgette)

1 whole head garlic

2 yellow onions, halved

✥ Preheat oven to 450°F (230°C/Gas Mark 6).

✥ For the marinade, in a shallow non-aluminum dish, combine all the marinade ingredients. Place hens in the dish, coat with marinade, cover, and refrigerate overnight, turning once.

✥ For the vegetables, cut the broccoli and cauliflower florets lengthwise into small florets. Cut the zucchini into quarters. Remove some outside layers of papery skin from the head of garlic and cut off the top one-fourth of the head, exposing the cloves.

✥ Arrange all vegetables in the bottom of a deep roasting pan. Pour in water to a depth of ⅛ inch (3 mm). Cover with aluminum foil. Place the pan in the center of the oven and immediately reduce the heat to 400°F (200°C/Gas Mark 5). Bake for 15 minutes.

✥ Remove pan from the oven, remove the foil, and rest a flat roasting rack over (not touching) the vegetables. Remove the hens from the marinade, reserving the marinade, and place them on the rack, skin-side down. Cook for a further 45 minutes.

✥ Remove the pan from oven and drain off excess liquid, leaving ⅛ inch (3 mm) in the bottom of the pan. Turn the vegetables over, then turn the hens, and baste with reserved marinade.

✥ Continue to roast until the hens are a deep brown and cooked through and the vegetables tender, about 30 minutes. (Check the vegetables during the last 15 minutes of roasting and remove them from the oven if done to your liking.)

✥ Remove the hens from the oven and let stand for 10 minutes before serving.

roast chicken
stuffed with
wild pecan rice

serves 6

Despite its name, wild pecan rice—a regional grain from Louisiana, U.S.A.—is not a type of rice, nor does it contain pecans. It has a rich nutty flavor and smells of popcorn as it cooks. If it is unavailable, substitute long grain rice and add pecans to the stuffing to give it a similarly nutty flavor.

1 cup (7 oz/220 g) wild pecan rice or long grain rice

chicken stock, as needed

1 tablespoon butter

½ fresh fennel bulb, chopped

2 green (spring) onions, chopped

½ cup (3½ oz/100 g) chopped pecans (optional)

⅓ cup (2 oz/60 g) dried cranberries or dried tart red cherries

¼ cup (⅓ oz/10 g) chopped fresh flatleaf (Italian) parsley

1 whole chicken, 3–3½ lb (1.5–1.8 kg)

1 tablespoon vegetable oil or melted butter

⟡ Preheat oven to 375°F (190°C/Gas Mark 4).

⟡ Prepare pecan rice according to package directions, except use chicken stock in place of water and omit salt. Or, bring 2 cups (16 fl oz/500 ml) of stock to a boil, add long grain rice, cover, and cook until rice is tender and liquid is absorbed, about 20 minutes. Set aside.

⟡ In a frying pan over medium heat, melt the 1 tablespoon butter. Add the fennel and green onion and cook, stirring, until tender, about 5 minutes. Stir in pecans (if using), cranberries or cherries, and parsley. Heat through and stir into the cooked rice.

⟡ Stuff the chicken with the rice mixture. Put any remaining stuffing into a 4-cup (1-qt/1-liter) casserole and cover with a lid or aluminum foil. Tie the chicken legs to tail, skewer neck skin to back, and twist the wings under the back. Place the chicken, breast-side up, on a rack in a shallow roasting pan. Brush the chicken with vegetable oil or melted butter. Roast until cooked through, 1¼–1½ hours. About 35 minutes before the end of the cooking time, place the covered casserole containing the extra stuffing into the oven.

⟡ When the chicken is done, cover loosely with aluminum foil and let stand in a warm place for 15 minutes before carving. Serve with the stuffing.

chicken
with lemon stuffing

serves 6

STUFFING

7 cups (3½ oz/100 g) dry bread cubes

1 small onion, finely chopped

2 teaspoons finely shredded lemon zest

½ teaspoon dried marjoram, crushed

½ teaspoon dried thyme, crushed

salt and pepper to taste

1 clove garlic, minced

1 egg, lightly beaten

½ cup (4 oz/125 g) butter, melted

3 tablespoons water

2 tablespoons lemon juice

ROAST CHICKEN

1 whole chicken, 3–3½ lb (1.5–1.8 kg)

1 tablespoon vegetable oil or melted butter

PAN GRAVY

¼ cup (1 oz/30 g) all-purpose (plain) flour

chicken stock or water

½ teaspoon finely shredded lemon zest

salt and pepper to taste

✤ Preheat oven to 375°F (190°C/Gas Mark 4).

✤ For the stuffing, in a large bowl, combine the bread cubes, onion, lemon zest, marjoram, thyme, salt and pepper, and garlic. In another bowl, stir together the egg, melted butter, water, and lemon juice. Drizzle this mixture over the bread cubes and toss to combine.

✤ For the roast chicken, stuff chicken and tie the legs to tail, skewer neck skin to back, and twist the wings under the back. Put any remaining stuffing into a 4-cup (1-qt/1-liter) casserole, drizzle with 1–2 tablespoons additional water, and cover with a lid or aluminum foil. Place the chicken, breast-side up, on a rack in a shallow roasting pan. Brush chicken with vegetable oil or melted butter. Roast until cooked through, 1¼–1½ hours. About 35 minutes before the end of the cooking time, place the covered casserole containing the extra stuffing into the oven.

✤ When the chicken is done, cover loosely with aluminum foil and let stand in a warm place for 15 minutes before carving.

✤ Meanwhile, prepare the pan gravy. Pour the chicken pan drippings into a large measuring cup and scrape up any browned bits from the bottom of the pan into the cup. Skim and reserve ¼ cup (2 fl oz/60 ml) fat from drippings and place into a saucepan (discard remaining fat, retaining rest of drippings). Stir in the flour and cook until gently bubbling. Add enough stock or water to the remaining drippings in the measuring cup to equal 2 cups (16 fl oz/500 ml). Add all at once to the flour mixture. Cook and stir over medium heat until thickened and bubbly. Add lemon zest and salt and pepper. Serve with the carved chicken.

roast chicken
with chile-cilantro butter

serves 6

Try to avoid direct contact with chiles. Wear plastic or rubber gloves to protect your skin while preparing them and, most importantly, avoid all contact with your eyes. Wash your hands thoroughly with soap and water when finished. Cilantro (fresh coriander) is the leafy part of the plant that gives us coriander seed.

4 cloves garlic, peeled

2 red chiles, coarsely chopped

1/4 cup (2 oz/60 g) butter, at room temperature

1 cup (1 oz/30 g) cilantro (fresh coriander)

1 whole chicken, 3–3 1/2 lb (1.5–1.8 kg)

paprika to taste

onion salt to taste

❖ Preheat oven to 375°F (190°C/Gas Mark 4).

❖ In a food processor or blender, finely chop the garlic cloves and red chiles. (Keep the lid closed while processing, and open carefully—do not inhale directly.) Add the butter and cilantro and process or blend until nearly smooth.

❖ Beginning at the neck of the bird, loosen the skin from the breast by working your fingers and thumb toward the tail. Loosen as much skin as possible without piercing the skin. Turn over and continue to loosen skin down both sides of the backbone, thighs, and legs. Spread the butter mixture, 1 tablespoon at a time, under the skin on the chicken breast and back. Rub your thumb on top of the skin to evenly distribute the mixture.

❖ Tie the legs to tail, skewer neck skin to back, and twist the wings under the back. Sprinkle with paprika and onion salt. Place chicken, breast-side up, on a rack in a shallow roasting pan. Roast until cooked through, 1¼–1½ hours. Cover loosely with aluminum foil and let stand in a warm place for 15 minutes before carving. Spoon pan juices over chicken and serve hot.

mint spice rub
chicken

serves 6

*1 whole chicken,
3–3 1/2 lb (1.5–1.8 kg)*

*2 teaspoons dried mint leaves,
crushed*

1 teaspoon ground cardamom

1/2 teaspoon ground cinnamon

salt and pepper to taste

*1 tablespoon vegetable oil or
olive oil*

✧ Preheat oven to 375°F (190°C/Gas Mark 4).

✧ Tie the chicken legs to tail, skewer neck skin to back, and twist the wings under the back. In a small mixing bowl, combine the mint, cardamom, cinnamon, and salt and pepper. Brush chicken with oil, then rub mint-spice mixture onto the skin.

✧ Place chicken, breast-side up, on a rack in a shallow roasting pan. Roast until cooked through, 1 1/4–1 1/2 hours. Cover loosely with aluminum foil and stand in a warm place for 15 minutes before carving. Serve hot.

stuffed chicken thighs

serves 6

¼ cup (2 oz/60 g) butter

2 leeks, finely chopped

1 garlic clove, crushed

2 tablespoons chopped fresh flatleaf
(Italian) parsley

3 tablespoons chopped tarragon

¾ cup (6 oz/185 g) cream cheese,
softened

¼ cup (1 oz/30 g) walnuts, chopped

6 chicken thighs
(about 1½ lb/750 g total)

2 tablespoons vegetable oil

2 teaspoons dried rosemary

◈ Preheat oven to 350°F (180°C/Gas 4).

◈ In a small frying pan over low heat, melt
1½ tablespoons of the butter. Add the leeks and
cook, stirring occasionally, until soft. Add garlic and
cook for 1 minute more. In a bowl, combine leek
mixture with the parsley, 1 tablespoon of the
tarragon, the cream cheese, and walnuts. Beat until
combined. Place an equal amount of cheese mixture
evenly under the skin of each chicken thigh. Place
the chicken on a rack in a roasting pan. Add the
remaining butter and the oil and bake until cooked
through, about 30 minutes, basting frequently.
Remove from the oven and sprinkle chicken with
the remaining tarragon and the rosemary.

chicken with
roasted garlic sauce

serves 6

While raw garlic is potent and sharp, when oven-roasted it develops a mellow, delicate sweetness that goes perfectly with roast chicken. The combination of roast chicken, garlic, and lemon juice is particularly flavorsome.

15 cloves garlic, peeled

1 whole chicken, 3–3½ lb (1.5–1.8 kg)

1 tablespoon minced garlic (about 6 cloves)

salt to taste

1 tablespoon vegetable oil

1 cup (8 fl oz/250 g) water

¼ cup (1 oz/30 g) all-purpose (plain) flour

chicken stock

1 tablespoon lemon juice

pepper

❖ Preheat oven to 375°F (190°C/Gas Mark 4).

❖ Flatten 5 of the garlic cloves and place inside the body cavity of the chicken. Tie the chicken legs to tail, skewer neck skin to back, and twist the wings under the back. Combine the minced garlic and salt. Brush chicken with oil, then rub garlic-salt mixture onto the skin.

❖ Place the chicken, breast-side up, on a rack in a shallow roasting pan. In another pan, combine the remaining garlic cloves and water. Place both pans in oven and roast, uncovered, until chicken is cooked through, 1¼–1½ hours. Spoon drippings over chicken occasionally. If necessary, to prevent overbrowning, cover chicken with aluminum foil for the last 20 minutes. Check garlic cloves frequently to be sure they have enough water to cook gently but not burn.

❖ When chicken is cooked, transfer to a serving platter. Cover loosely with aluminum foil and let stand in a warm place for 15 minutes before carving.

❖ Meanwhile, make the gravy. Pour the chicken pan drippings into a large measuring cup and scrape up any browned bits from the bottom of the pan into the cup. Skim and reserve ¼ cup (2 fl oz/60 ml) fat from drippings and place into a saucepan (discard remaining fat, retaining rest of drippings). Stir in flour and cook, stirring, until flour is golden, about 2 minutes. To the remaining drippings in the measuring cup, add the cooked garlic cloves, their cooking water, and enough stock to equal 2 cups (16 fl oz/500 ml). Add all at once to flour mixture. Cook, stirring, over medium heat until thick and bubbling. Continue to cook, stirring, for a further 2 minutes. Stir in lemon juice and pepper just before serving. Serve with the carved chicken.

prosciutto and chicken frittata

serves 4–6

Potatoes are a wonderfully versatile vegetable. New potatoes have a crisp, waxy texture because their sugar hasn't yet converted fully to starch. You can use any variety of young potato for this recipe. Choose firm, well-rounded potatoes without any green tinges or signs of wrinkling.

3 tablespoons butter

8 baby new potatoes, thinly sliced

1 red (Spanish) onion, sliced

3 oz (90 g) prosciutto, thinly sliced

10 oz (315 g) cooked chicken meat, shredded

1/3 cup (1 1/2 oz/40 g) drained, oil-packed, sun-dried tomatoes, sliced

8 eggs, lightly beaten

salt and pepper to taste

1/2 cup (2 oz/60 g) grated Parmesan cheese

1 cup (3 oz/90 g) shredded Jarlsberg cheese

1/2 cup (1/2 oz/15 g) shredded fresh basil

In a 10-inch (25-cm) nonstick frying pan over medium-high heat, warm 2 tablespoons of the butter and add the potatoes. Cook, turning occasionally, until golden brown and tender, about 15 minutes. Remove potatoes from pan. In the pan, heat the remaining 1 tablespoon butter, add the onion and prosciutto, and cook, stirring, until the onion is soft. Return the potatoes to the pan, mix well, and press the mixture flat. Top with the chicken and tomatoes.

In a bowl, combine the eggs, salt and pepper, cheeses, and basil and mix well. Gently pour the egg mixture over the mixture in the pan. Over low heat, cook until the base is golden, about 10 minutes. Place the pan under a hot broiler (griller) to set and brown the top of the frittata.

Loosen the edges of the frittata and turn out onto a plate or board. Cut into wedges and serve.

time saving

This recipe can be made up to a day ahead and is perfect for picnics or a light lunch.

stuffed
chicken breasts
with bell pepper coulis

serves 4

STUFFED CHICKEN BREASTS

3 oz (90 g) cream cheese, at room
temperature

2 tablespoons grated Parmesan cheese

1 tablespoon drained capers

1 tablespoon milk

1 clove garlic, minced

pepper to taste

4 skinless, boneless chicken breast halves
(1 lb/500 g total)

1 tablespoon olive oil or vegetable oil

1/4 cup (2 fl oz/60 ml) dry white wine

BELL PEPPER COULIS

2 red bell peppers (capsicums), roasted and
peeled, or 1 x 6-oz (185-g) jar roasted bell
peppers, drained

1 tablespoon olive oil or vegetable oil

2 cloves garlic, minced

1/4 cup (2 fl oz/60 ml) half-and-half (half
cream) or light (single) cream

2 teaspoons anchovy paste

1 tablespoon drained capers

✥ Preheat oven to 350°F (180°C/Gas Mark 4).

✥ For the chicken breasts, in a small mixing bowl, combine the cream cheese, Parmesan cheese, capers, milk, garlic, and pepper. Set aside.

✥ Place each breast half between plastic wrap. Working from the center to the edges, pound chicken with the flat side of a meat mallet to ⅛ inch (3 mm) thick. Remove plastic wrap. Spread one-fourth of the cream cheese mixture over each breast half. Fold in the sides and roll up, jelly-roll (Swiss-roll) style, pressing the edges to seal.

✥ In a large frying pan over medium-high heat, warm the oil. Add the chicken and brown on both sides, about 5 minutes total. Transfer chicken to an 8-cup (2-qt/2-l) baking dish. Pour the wine over the chicken and bake, uncovered, until cooked through, 20–25 minutes.

✥ For the coulis, in a blender or food processor, blend or process the bell peppers until smooth. Set aside. In a small saucepan over medium heat, warm the remaining oil. Add the garlic and cook, stirring, until tender but not brown, about 2 minutes. Add the puréed bell peppers, half-and-half or cream, anchovy paste, and capers. Heat through. Divide the coulis between four warmed serving plates and top each with a chicken breast. Serve hot.

oregano and lemon chicken

serves 4

When Greek cooks roast chicken, they will likely produce this venerable taverna dish, in which the accompanying potatoes become especially tender, juicy, and lemony. Serve with white wine and a zesty Greek salad.

1 whole chicken, about 5 lb (2.5 kg)

1 lemon, quartered

1/2 cup (4 fl oz/125 ml) olive oil

salt and ground black pepper to taste

12 cloves garlic, 4 peeled, 8 unpeeled and crushed

2 teaspoons dried oregano, plus 3 tablespoons extra

1/3 cup (2 1/2 fl oz/80 ml) fresh lemon juice

2 teaspoons coarsely cracked black pepper

6 white boiling potatoes, peeled and cut into large wedges

1 cup (8 fl oz/250 ml) water or chicken stock, or as needed

1/4 cup (1/3 oz/10 g) chopped fresh flatleaf (Italian) parsley

❖ Preheat oven to 400°F (200°C/Gas Mark 5). Rub the chicken inside and out with the lemon quarters and 1–2 tablespoons of the oil. Sprinkle with salt and pepper. Place the lemon quarters, peeled garlic cloves, and the 2 teaspoons oregano in the chicken body cavity. Tie the chicken legs to tail, skewer neck skin to back, and twist the wings under the back. Place the chicken on a rack in a roasting pan.

❖ In a small saucepan, combine the remaining oil, the lemon juice, 2 tablespoons of the oregano, cracked pepper, and salt. Simmer for 3 minutes. Remove pan from heat and set aside.

❖ Place potatoes around chicken and sprinkle with the remaining oregano and the crushed garlic cloves. Spoon a little of the lemon-oil mixture over the chicken. Pour 1 cup (8 fl oz/ 250 ml) water or stock evenly over the potatoes and place in oven. Roast for 15 minutes. Baste the chicken with some of the lemon-oil mixture and reduce the heat to 350°F (180°C/ Gas Mark 4). Roast the chicken, basting with the lemon-oil mixture every 10–15 minutes, until cooked through, about 1 hour more. Transfer chicken to a warmed serving platter, cover loosely with aluminum foil, and let stand in a warm place for 15 minutes. If the potatoes aren't golden brown, increase the heat to 450°F (220°C/Gas Mark 6) and cook for a further 15–20 minutes, adding more water or stock, if needed, to prevent sticking.

❖ Arrange the potatoes around the chicken. Using a large spoon, skim off the fat from the roasting pan, then pour the pan juices into a small serving pitcher. Sprinkle the chicken and potatoes with the parsley. Carve the chicken and pass the pan juices at the table.

poussins
with vegetable stuffing

serves 4

2 tablespoons butter

1 cup (6 oz/185 g) finely chopped carrots

1 cup (4 oz/125 g) finely chopped celery

1/3 cup (1 1/2 oz/40 g) finely chopped leek

1/2 cup (2 1/2 oz/75 g) sliced fresh mushrooms

1/2 cup (2 oz/60 g) finely chopped onion

1/2 teaspoon dried thyme, crushed

salt and pepper to taste

1/4 cup (2 fl oz/60 ml) light (single) cream
(optional)

2 poussins (spatchcocks) or Cornish game
hens, each about 1–1 1/2 lb (500-750 g)

1 tablespoon vegetable oil

❖ Preheat oven to 375°F (190°C/Gas Mark 4).

❖ In a large frying pan over medium heat, melt the butter. Add the carrots, celery, leek, mushrooms, and onion and cook until crisp-tender but not brown, about 5 minutes. Add thyme, salt, and pepper. If desired, stir in cream to moisten. Cool vegetable mixture slightly.

❖ Spoon some of the vegetable mixture loosely into the body cavity of each poussin. Tie the legs to tail, skewer neck skin to back, and twist the wings under the back. Put any remaining stuffing into a small casserole, cover, and chill. Place the birds, breast-side up, on a rack in a shallow roasting pan. Brush with oil. Cover loosely with aluminum foil. Bake for 20 minutes. Uncover birds and bake until cooked through, a further 20–25 minutes. Place casserole with remaining stuffing in the oven for the last 20 minutes of roasting. Remove birds from the oven, cover loosely with aluminum foil, and allow to stand for 15 minutes before serving. To serve, cut each bird in half. Serve with the stuffing.

recipe variations

This is a great recipe with lots of room for you to add your own personal variation. Try this with a tasty roasting chicken and experiment. For an Italian flavor, for example, use pine nuts and Parmesan cheese instead of the carrots and celery. Alternatively, replace the dried thyme with a large bunch of fresh, finely chopped basil.

frying

and sautéing

frying and sautéing basics

There are various methods of frying. Pan frying uses a small amount of fat, unlike deep frying, which uses much more. Sautéing is often considered the same as pan frying, but it uses even less fat and is a quicker method of cooking. When done correctly, pan frying and sautéing should not be greasy and should result in chicken that is tender, juicy, and full of flavor.

Pan frying generally has a barrier between the food and the fat—usually flour, then a liquid, such as milk, and then another dry layer, such as bread crumbs or more flour. This coating adds texture, flavor, and color, producing a wonderfully tasty, crunchy exterior. It is best for smaller chicken pieces with the bone still in. Sautéing is best for boneless pieces of chicken, with or without a coating. If there is a coating, it usually consists just of seasoned flour. (Stir-frying is an even quicker technique than pan frying, and uses smaller pieces of food cut to a uniform size. It is usually done in a wok, but can be done in a frying pan.)

Temperature control is essential for well-cooked chicken that is nicely browned and evenly cooked all the way through. The single most important tool for successful pan frying and sautéing is a good, heavy-based frying pan. A heavy-based frying pan is responsive to changes in heat, evenly distributes heat, and also retains heat well. All these factors are essential in pan frying or sautéing because the most common problem is burnt and unevenly cooked chicken.

frying and sautéing basics

Use a frying pan that is large enough to hold a number of pieces of chicken. Be sure, too, that the handle stays cool and comfortable to hold. (Always keep the handle turned away from you to avoid knocking it and spilling the hot food.)

Other tools for pan frying and sautéing are tongs, for turning and removing the chicken pieces, and a strong plastic bag, for coating several chicken pieces at one time.

For the best results when pan frying and sautéing, before adding the chicken pieces to the pan, heat the fat on medium heat until hot. With tongs, place the chicken in the pan. Make sure you leave room between pieces so all sides are exposed to the fat. Cook until one side is evenly browned, about 10 minutes, depending on the size of the pieces. When one side is done, turn the pieces to brown on the other side. Reduce the heat to medium-low and cook until chicken is cooked through.

By pounding chicken breasts into thin rectangles, you can add all sorts of fillings and roll up the pieces ready for cooking. Pound the chicken by placing the pieces between plastic wrap and, with the flat side of a meat mallet, starting from the center and working outward, gently pound the chicken to ¼ inch (6 mm) thick. Pounding is also useful to even out the thickness of the chicken pieces to ensure even cooking.

To deep-fry chicken pieces, in a wok or saucepan, use enough oil to completely cover and surround the pieces you are cooking. Heat the oil to 365°F (185°C) (use a deep-fat thermometer to test temperature). The correct temperature is very important, otherwise the food will absorb fat, become greasy, and even burn. When deep frying, always fill the pan or wok only halfway with oil, to avoid fat splashing out of the pan and possibly catching fire. Always lift food out with tongs or a slotted spoon and drain on paper towels to absorb any excess oil.

potato rosti with chicken

serves 4

3 tablespoons vegetable oil

1 onion, chopped

1 clove garlic, crushed

4 large potatoes,
peeled and coarsely grated

3 tablespoons butter

salt and pepper to taste

2 tablespoons corn relish

2 tablespoons salsa
(tomato and chile pickle)

1 lb (500 g) cooked chicken meat,
sliced

2 small ripe tomatoes,
finely chopped

¼ cup (2 fl oz/60 ml) sour cream

2 tablespoons chopped
fresh chives

◈ In a large frying pan over medium-high heat, warm half the oil. Add onion and garlic and cook, stirring, until onion is soft. Add potatoes and cook, stirring, until soft and sticky, about 15 minutes. Cool slightly.

◈ In a small frying pan over medium heat, warm one-fourth of the remaining oil and one-fourth of the butter. Add one-fourth of the potato mixture and press into a round 6 inches (15 cm) in diameter. Cook on both sides until well browned and crisp. Remove from the pan, sprinkle with salt and pepper, and keep warm. Repeat with the remaining potato mixture, oil, and butter to make three more rounds.

◈ In a saucepan over medium heat, combine corn relish and salsa and cook, stirring, until heated through.

◈ Top the rosti with the chicken, tomatoes, salsa mixture, sour cream, and chives. Serve immediately.

spring rolls

serves 4–6 as an appetizer

Spring rolls were traditionally served during the Chinese Spring Festival. They were originally assembled by the diners at the table. The wrappers would be served along with a variety of pork, chicken, or vegetables for the filling, and each person would make his or her own rolls, which would then be heated individually. This recipe is much simpler.

MARINADE

2 teaspoons light soy sauce

1 teaspoon oyster sauce

1 teaspoon cornstarch (cornflour)

SPRING ROLLS

4 oz (125 g) chicken breast meat, shredded

4 cups (1 qt/1 liter) groundnut (peanut) oil

2 dried black mushrooms, soaked, drained, stems discarded, and shredded

4 oz (125 g) bamboo shoots, shredded

2 oz (60 g) chives, cut into 1-inch (2.5-cm) lengths

16 spring roll wrappers

For the marinade, in a bowl, mix the soy sauce, oyster sauce, and cornstarch. Add the chicken and marinate for 15 minutes.

In a wok or frying pan over medium heat, warm 1–2 tablespoons of oil. Add undrained chicken and the mushrooms and cook for 1 minute. Add bamboo shoots and cook for 30 seconds more. Mix in the chives. Transfer to a dish and let cool. Drain off any liquid.

Place one spring roll wrapper on a flat surface and place a portion of the filling in the center. Fold both ends toward the center. Fold up the lower flap and roll the wrapper into a tube shape. Wet the end flap with water and seal. Repeat with remaining wrappers.

In a pan or wok, heat the remaining oil until hot. Add the rolls, a few at a time, and fry until golden brown, about 30 seconds. Remove, drain, and serve.

recipe variations

You can try this recipe with a combination of chicken and peanuts or other nuts. Use half the quantity of chicken and add 2 oz (60 g) of coarsely chopped nuts when you add the bamboo shoots. Or, try adding chile to the marinade—make it as hot or as mild as you like.

spicy chinese chicken balls

makes about 70 balls
serves 10 as an appetizer

1 lb (500 g) ground (minced) chicken

3 cups (6 oz/180 g) stale bread crumbs

1 egg, lightly beaten

4 green (spring) onions, chopped

2 cloves garlic, crushed

2 tablespoons soy sauce

2 tablespoons hoisin sauce

1 teaspoon peeled and grated fresh ginger

1 teaspoon sesame oil

2 tablespoons sesame seeds

vegetable oil, for deep-frying

DIPPING SAUCE

2 tablespoons soy sauce

2 tablespoons sweet chile sauce

1 tablespoon dry sherry

In a bowl, combine the chicken, bread crumbs, egg, green onions, garlic, soy sauce, hoisin sauce, ginger, sesame oil, and sesame seeds. Mix well and shape mixture into balls, 2 level teaspoons at a time.

Heat the oil to 350°F (180°C) and fry the balls, a few at a time, until well browned and cooked through, about 4 minutes—do not have the oil too hot or the balls will not cook through. Remove from the pan and drain on paper towels. Keep warm while cooking the remaining balls in the same way.

For the dipping sauce, in a bowl, combine all the ingredients and mix well.

Serve hot chicken balls with the dipping sauce.

recipe hint

This recipe can be made a day ahead. Reheat the balls on a baking sheet in a preheated 350°F (180°C/Gas Mark 4) oven, for about 10 minutes.

cumin pancake stacks with guacamole

makes 12 pancakes

serves 4

2 red bell peppers (capsicums), quartered

CUMIN PANCAKES

1 teaspoon cumin seeds

2 cups (10 oz/315 g) all-purpose (plain) flour

1 teaspoon baking soda (bicarbonate of soda)

1 tablespoon sugar

3 eggs, separated

2 cups (16 fl oz/500 ml) buttermilk

¼ cup (2 oz/60 g) butter, melted

1 x 12-oz (375-g) can corn kernels, drained

4 bacon strips (rashers)

2 ripe avocados

2 tablespoons chopped cilantro (fresh coriander)

1 tablespoon taco (chile) sauce, plus extra

2 teaspoons lime juice

salt and pepper to taste

1 lb (500 g) cooked chicken meat, sliced

2 tomatoes, chopped

⅓ cup (3 fl oz/90 ml) sour cream

1 tablespoon packed chopped cilantro (fresh coriander)

❖ Broil (grill) the bell peppers, skin side up, until the skin blisters and blackens, about 10 minutes. Place the hot bell peppers in a plastic bag, seal, and leave for 10 minutes. (The steam created will loosen the skins, making the peppers easier to peel.) Peel and slice thinly.

❖ For the pancakes, in a dry frying pan over medium heat, toast the cumin seeds until fragrant, being careful not to burn them, about 2 minutes.

❖ In a large mixing bowl, sift the flour and baking soda. Stir through the sugar. In a small mixing bowl, combine the egg yolks, buttermilk, and butter. Add to the flour mixture and whisk until smooth. Stir in the corn and cumin seeds. (Or, if you prefer, process the above ingredients, except the corn, in a food processor. Then stir in the corn.)

❖ In a small mixing bowl, using an electric mixer on medium to high speed, beat the egg whites until soft peaks form. Fold into batter in two batches.

❖ Spoon ½ cup (4 fl oz/125 ml) of the pancake mixture into a heated greased frying pan and cook over medium heat until golden brown underneath and the bubbles begin to burst on the top. Turn the pancake and cook until browned on the other side and set. Remove the pancake from the pan and keep warm. Repeat with the remaining batter to make 12 pancakes.

❖ Remove the rind from the bacon and cut each slice in half. In a dry frying pan, cook the bacon until just crisp.

✧ In a bowl, combine the avocados, cilantro, taco sauce, and lime juice. Using a fork, mash well. Add salt and pepper.

✧ Place one pancake on each plate and top it with some of the avocado mixture, chicken, bell pepper, bacon, and tomatoes. Drizzle with extra taco sauce. Repeat, making another layer, then top the lot with a third pancake. Top with sour cream and cilantro if desired. Assemble the remaining three servings and serve immediately.

recipe hint

These pancakes are best made close to serving. The batter can be prepared up to a day ahead and cooked just before serving.

the works
mexican burger

serves 4

1/3 cup (2 1/3 fl oz/80 ml) vegetable oil

2 onions, thinly sliced

1/2 teaspoon ground cumin

1 large avocado

2 teaspoons lime juice

salt and pepper to taste

1 x 15-oz (425-g) can refried beans

BURGERS

1 1/2 lb (750 g) ground (minced) chicken

1 tablespoon chopped cilantro (fresh coriander)

1 tablespoon ground cumin

1 teaspoon salt

1/4 teaspoon chile powder

2 cloves garlic, crushed

6 green (spring) onions, chopped

2 1/2 cups (5 oz/150 g) stale bread crumbs

1 egg, lightly beaten

1 x 6-oz (185-g) package corn chips

1/2 head romaine (cos) lettuce, shredded

1 cup (8 fl oz/250 ml) prepared chunky-style salsa (tomato and chile pickle)

1/3 cup (3 fl oz/90 ml) sour cream

cilantro (fresh coriander) sprigs

1/3 cup (3 fl oz/90 ml) chile sauce

the works mexican burger

Stale bread crumbs are made from one- to two-day-old bread—do not substitute dried packaged bread crumbs. Stale bread crumbs can be made in large quantities in the food processor and frozen in 1-cup (2-oz/60-g) bags for convenience.

✦ In a frying pan over medium heat, warm half the oil. Add the onions and cook, stirring, until soft, 3 minutes. Add the cumin and cook, stirring, until fragrant.

✦ In a small bowl, combine the avocado with the lime juice and salt and pepper. Using a fork, mash well. Put in an airtight container until ready to use.

✦ In a saucepan, heat the refried beans.

✦ For the burgers, in a bowl, combine the chicken, cilantro, cumin, salt, chile powder, garlic, green onions, 1½ cups (3 oz/90 g) of the bread crumbs, and the egg. Mix well. Shape the mixture into four large flat patties, about 1 inch (2.5 cm) thick. Press the remaining bread crumbs onto the patties and refrigerate for 1 hour.

the works mexican burger

❖ In a large frying pan over medium-low heat, warm the remaining oil and cook the burger patties until well browned and cooked through, about 5 minutes on each side.

❖ Arrange the corn chips around the edge of each plate and pile the lettuce in the center of each plate. Top with a burger, then some of the beans, onions, salsa, avocado, sour cream, and cilantro. Drizzle with the chile sauce and serve.

recipe hint

This recipe can be prepared a day ahead—reheat and assemble just before serving. The uncooked patties are suitable for freezing.

beer barbecue
chicken legs

serves 4

2 lb (1 kg) chicken drumsticks
and/or thighs, skinned if
desired

1 tablespoon vegetable oil

1/3 cup (2½ oz/80 g)
chopped onion

1/2 cup (4 fl oz/125 ml)
chile sauce

1/2 cup (4 fl oz/125 ml) beer

2 tablespoons brown sugar

1/2 teaspoon ground cumin

1/2 teaspoon prepared mustard

pepper to taste

few drops hot pepper sauce

✣ In a large frying pan over medium heat, warm
the oil. Add the chicken and cook, uncovered, turning
to brown evenly, about 10–15 minutes total. Drain off
the fat. Add the onion and cook for 2–3 minutes more.

✣ In a small mixing bowl, combine the chile sauce,
beer, sugar, cumin, mustard, pepper, and hot pepper
sauce. Pour mixture over the chicken. Bring to a boil,
then reduce heat, cover, and simmer for 20 minutes.
Uncover and turn chicken. Simmer, uncovered, until
chicken is cooked through, a further 10–15 minutes.
Transfer chicken to a serving dish and keep warm.

✣ Skim excess fat off sauce in pan. Simmer sauce,
uncovered, until reduced to desired consistency.
Serve the sauce with the chicken.

chicken with sauce suprême

serves 4

2 tablespoons butter

4 skinless, boneless chicken breast halves (1 lb/500 g total)

salt and pepper to taste

½ cup (2½ oz/75 g) sliced fresh mushrooms

2 finely chopped shallots

¼ cup (2 fl oz/60 ml) dry white wine

1 cup (8 fl oz/250 ml) chicken stock

2 tablespoons all-purpose (plain) flour

2 teaspoons chopped fresh thyme

1 bay leaf

3 tablespoons heavy (double) cream

◈ In a large frying pan over medium heat, melt the butter. Add the chicken and cook until cooked through, turning once, 10–15 minutes total. Add salt and pepper and transfer to a serving dish. Keep warm.

◈ In the same frying pan, in the chicken drippings, cook the mushrooms and shallots until tender, about 3 minutes. Spoon over chicken and keep warm. To the pan, add the wine, stirring to loosen any crusty browned bits in the bottom of the pan. Stir together the stock, flour, thyme, and bay leaf. Add to the pan. Cook, stirring, until the sauce is thick and bubbly. Cook for a further 2 minutes. Stir in the cream. Remove the bay leaf and add salt and pepper.

◈ Serve the chicken and sauce tossed through hot cooked pasta.

chicken calvados

1 tablespoon vegetable oil

4 skinless, boneless chicken breast
halves (1 lb/500 g total)

3 tablespoons butter

2 tablespoons packed brown sugar

2 small apples, peeled and sliced

1 cup (8 fl oz/250 ml)
clear apple juice

1/2 cup (4 fl oz/125 ml) chicken stock

1 tablespoon cornstarch (cornflour)
blended with 1 tablespoon cold water

1/4 cup (2 fl oz/60 ml)
heavy (double) cream

1 tablespoon chopped fresh chervil
sprigs (chives may be substituted)

2 tablespoons Calvados or brandy

✧ In a large frying pan over medium-high heat,
warm the oil. Add the chicken and cook until well
browned and cooked through, 10–15 minutes.
Remove from the pan and keep warm.

✧ Drain any excess oil from the pan. Add the
butter and sugar and heat until butter is melted.
Add the apples and cook until lightly browned,
about 5 minutes. With a slotted spoon, remove
apples from the pan. Add the apple juice and
simmer until reduced by about one-third. Add
stock and cornstarch mixture and cook, stirring
constantly, until mixture is thick and bubbling.
Stir in cream, chervil, and apples.

✧ In a small saucepan over low heat, heat the
Calvados or brandy. Carefully ignite and pour
over the sauce. Serve the chicken with the sauce.

tarragon and lemon
marinated
chicken breasts

serves 4

juice of 1 lemon

2 tablespoons vegetable oil

pepper to taste

2 teaspoons dried tarragon

4 skinless, boneless chicken
breast halves (1 lb/500 g total)

fresh tarragon sprigs

lemon slices

❖ In a screwtop jar, combine the lemon juice, oil, pepper, and dried tarragon and shake vigorously. Place the chicken in a glass or ceramic bowl and pour the mixture over the chicken. Marinate for 20 minutes.

❖ In a large frying pan over medium heat, cook the undrained chicken until cooked through, turning once, 10–12 minutes total. Transfer to warmed plates and garnish with fresh tarragon and lemon slices.

❖ NOTE Chicken can be marinated, covered, in the refrigerator, up to several hours in advance, if desired.

basil chicken
with risotto
and chile-tomato coulis

serves 6

CHILE-TOMATO COULIS

1 tablespoon olive oil

1 onion, chopped

1 clove garlic, crushed

1 large can (1¾ lb/875 g) plum tomatoes

1 tablespoon tomato paste

1½ tablespoons sweet chile sauce

RISOTTO

2 tablespoons olive oil

1 large onion, chopped

1 clove garlic, crushed

1½ cups (10 oz/315 g) arborio rice

pinch saffron or ¼ teaspoon turmeric

½ cup (4 fl oz/125 ml) dry white wine

4 cups (32 fl oz/1 liter) hot chicken stock

3 tablespoons butter

⅓ cup (1 oz/30 g) grated Parmesan cheese

2 tablespoons olive oil

6 skinless, boneless chicken breast halves
(1½ lb/750 g total)

2 tablespoons butter

2 tablespoons chopped fresh basil

❖ For the coulis, in a saucepan over medium-high heat, warm the oil. Add the onion and garlic and cook, stirring, until the onion is soft, about 3 minutes. Add the undrained tomatoes and simmer, uncovered, until pulpy, about 5 minutes. Blend or process the mixture until just smooth—do not over-process or the sauce will become orange rather than red. Press the mixture through a sieve and discard the pulp. Stir in the tomato paste and sweet chile sauce and simmer, uncovered, until the mixture has reduced to about 2 cups (16 fl oz/500 ml).

❖ For the risotto, in a medium saucepan over medium-high heat, warm the oil. Add the onion and garlic and cook, stirring, until the onion is soft. Add the rice and saffron and stir until the rice is well coated. Add the wine and ¼ cup (2 fl oz/60 ml) of hot stock. Simmer, stirring, until all of the liquid is absorbed. Add the remaining stock in about four batches, stirring until each batch of liquid is absorbed before adding more. Total cooking time should be about 20 minutes, or until the rice is tender. Finally, stir in the butter and cheese.

❖ Meanwhile, in a large frying pan over medium-high heat, warm the oil. Add the chicken and cook until well browned and cooked through, turning once, 10–15 minutes total. Slice the chicken diagonally, return to the pan with the butter and basil, and stir until well combined.

❖ Divide the coulis between the plates and top with the risotto then the chicken mixture.

spiced lime chicken salad

serves 6

2 tablespoons vegetable oil

6 skinless, boneless chicken breast halves
(1½ lb/750 g total)

1 tablespoon ground cumin

2 carrots

1 cup (7 oz/220 g) fresh asparagus,
chopped

1 cup (7 oz/220 g) sugar snap peas

1 cup (5 oz/150 g) bean sprouts

1 red bell pepper (capsicum), thinly sliced

1 head romaine (cos) lettuce, torn

1 onion, thinly sliced

DRESSING

¾ cup (6 fl oz/190 ml) vegetable oil

1 teaspoon grated lime zest

½ cup (4 fl oz/125 ml) lime juice

¼ cup (¼ oz/8 g) chopped cilantro (fresh
coriander)

2 teaspoons chopped fresh chile

2 tablespoons Thai fish sauce

1 tablespoon sugar

3 cloves garlic, crushed

2 tablespoons chopped fresh mint

❖ In a frying pan over medium-high heat, warm the oil. Sprinkle the chicken with cumin, add to the pan, and cook until chicken is well browned and cooked through, turning once, 10–15 minutes total. Remove from the pan and cut into thick slices.

❖ With a vegetable peeler, peel the carrots lengthwise into strips. In a bowl of cold water, add the carrot peel and let stand until crisp, about 30 minutes. In a small saucepan, boil the asparagus and peas until just tender, 4 minutes. Drain and refresh in iced water. Drain again.

❖ For the dressing, in a screw-top jar, combine the oil, lime zest and juice, cilantro, chile, fish sauce, sugar, garlic, and mint. Shake well.

❖ In a bowl, combine the warm chicken with the vegetables, sprouts, lettuce, and onion and toss. Drizzle with dressing just before serving.

recipe **hint**

To make this a really fast meal, buy a hot cooked chicken and use the meat. Make double the amount of dressing and refrigerate until needed. You could use this dressing for any salad.

warm chicken and bell pepper salad

serves 4

2 tablespoons olive oil

2 tablespoons butter

4 skinless, boneless chicken breast halves
(1 lb/500 g total)

1 each of red, green, and yellow bell
peppers (capsicum)

DRESSING

1/2 cup (1 3/4 oz/50 g) walnuts

1/3 cup (2 1/2 fl oz/80 ml) walnut oil

1/4 cup (2 fl oz/60 ml) olive oil

1/4 cup (2 fl oz/60 ml) lemon juice

1 tablespoon fresh thyme leaves

1 tablespoon honey

❖ In a frying pan over medium-high heat, warm the oil and butter. Add the chicken and cook on both sides until well browned and cooked through, 10–15 minutes total. Remove the chicken from the pan and slice.

❖ Quarter the bell peppers and broil (grill), skin-side up, until the skin blisters and blackens. Peel and slice thickly.

❖ For the dressing, in a saucepan over low heat, combine all of the ingredients and stir until the honey has dissolved.

❖ Arrange chicken and bell peppers on plates and sprinkle with salt and pepper. Drizzle with dressing and serve warm.

chicken antipasto

serves 4–6 as a light lunch

½ cup (4 fl oz/125 ml) olive oil

1 tablespoon balsamic vinegar

2 tablespoons chopped fresh basil

2 cloves garlic, crushed

1½ lb (750 g) chicken breast meat,
sliced lengthwise in strips

2 x 6-oz (185-g) jars marinated
artichoke hearts

1 cup (3 oz/90 g) small white (button)
mushrooms

½ cup (4 oz/125 g) black olives

3 oz (90 g) bocconcini (mozzarella balls),
drained

12 baby radishes, trimmed

2 loaves focaccia, sliced into wedges

¼ cup (4 oz/125 g) pesto

Italian bread sticks (grissini)
or crusty Italian bread

❖ In a small bowl, combine 3 fl oz (100 ml) of oil, the vinegar, basil, and garlic. Mix well.

❖ In a frying pan over medium-high heat, warm the remaining oil. Add the chicken and cook, stirring, until cooked through, 10–15 minutes. Pour ¼ cup (2 fl oz/60 ml) of the oil mixture over the chicken. Cool, then refrigerate for several hours.

❖ In a bowl, combine the artichokes and mushrooms. Pour on remaining oil mixture. Cover and refrigerate for several hours.

❖ Arrange the chicken, artichoke hearts, mushrooms, olives, bocconcini, and radishes on a platter. Toast the focaccia until lightly browned and spread with the pesto. Serve with bread sticks or crusty bread.

greek-style
chicken salad

serves 4

4 skinless, boneless chicken breast halves
(1 lb/500 g total)

¼ cup (2 fl oz/60 ml) lemon juice

2 tablespoons olive oil plus ¼ cup
(2 fl oz/60 ml) extra

1 tablespoon honey

2 cloves garlic, crushed

2 tablespoons chopped fresh rosemary

1 tablespoon grain mustard

1 eggplant (aubergine), thinly sliced

1 bunch (1¼ lb/625 g) leaf (English) spinach

2 tomatoes, thinly sliced

1 onion, thinly sliced

¼ cup (2 oz/60 g) black (Riviera) olives

5 oz (150 g) feta cheese, cubed

¼ cup (2 fl oz/60 ml) extra-virgin olive oil

◈ In a shallow, non-metallic dish, combine the chicken, lemon juice, 2 tablespoons olive oil, honey, garlic, rosemary, and mustard. Cover and refrigerate for several hours or overnight. Drain the marinade from the chicken and reserve.

◈ In a frying pan over medium heat, warm the remaining ¼ cup (2 fl oz/60 g) olive oil. Add the eggplant in batches and cook until lightly browned and tender. Drain on paper towels.

◈ To the frying pan, add the chicken and cook until well browned and cooked through, 10–15 minutes. Take care not to burn the chicken, as honey causes it to brown quickly. Remove from pan and slice.

◈ Arrange the chicken, eggplant, spinach, tomatoes, onion, olives, and cheese on a serving plate or bowl. To the pan, add the reserved marinade and bring to a boil. Cool, then add the extra-virgin olive oil and spoon over the chicken and salad. Serve immediately.

warm thai
chicken salad

serves 6 as an appetizer or light lunch

MARINADE AND CHICKEN

1/4 cup (2 fl oz/60 ml) fresh lemon juice

salt to taste

2 cloves garlic, crushed

1 tablespoon brown sugar

2 tablespoons finely chopped cilantro
(fresh coriander)

6 skinless, boneless chicken breast halves
(1 1/2 lb/750 g total), sliced into four pieces

DRESSING

1 small red chile, finely chopped

1 clove garlic, finely chopped

3 tablespoons extra-virgin olive oil

1 tablespoon balsamic vinegar

juice of 2 limes

1 teaspoon sweet chile sauce

SALAD

1 bunch (14 oz/440 g) mizuna or other
salad leaves

1 red bell pepper (capsicum), julienned

1 cucumber, julienned

2 carrots, julienned

6 green (spring) onions, sliced

1 cup (1 oz/30 g) loosely packed cilantro
(fresh coriander) sprigs

1 cup (1 oz/30 g) shredded purple basil

3 tablespoons sesame oil

3 tablespoons toasted sesame seeds

In a shallow, non-metallic bowl, combine the marinade ingredients and mix well. Add the chicken and toss to coat. Cover with plastic wrap and refrigerate for several hours or overnight.

For the dressing, in a small bowl, combine the chile, garlic, oil, vinegar, lime juice, and chile sauce. Whisk until well combined.

For the salad, divide the mizuna, bell pepper, cucumber, carrots, green onions, cilantro, and basil among individual serving plates.

In a wok or frying pan over medium-high heat, warm the sesame oil until smoking. Cook the chicken until cooked through, about 3 minutes. Divide the chicken among the serving plates. Drizzle on the dressing and sprinkle with the toasted sesame seeds.

Serve while the chicken is still warm.

recipe hint

To achieve evenly cooked chicken, gently pound each breast half to an even thickness before slicing into four. Make sure you don't pound them too thin or they will dry out during cooking— pound them just enough to even out the really thick parts. Take extra care when cutting the chicken into four pieces— make these as uniformly sized as possible, as this will also help with even cooking.

filled breasts in mushroom-wine sauce

serves 4

FILLING

2 teaspoons butter

2 tablespoons finely chopped yellow onion

1 teaspoon minced garlic

3/4 lb (375 g) spinach leaves

3 tablespoons drained, chopped, oil-packed, sun-dried tomatoes

2 tablespoons grated Parmesan cheese

salt and pepper to taste

4 skinless, boneless chicken breast halves (1 lb/500 g total)

4 thin slices Emmenthaler cheese

2 tablespoons canola oil

1/2 cup (2 1/2 oz/75 g) all-purpose (plain) flour

MUSHROOM-WINE SAUCE

2 teaspoons unsalted butter

1/2 yellow onion, thinly sliced

1/2 lb (250 g) fresh white (button) mushrooms, stems removed, caps thinly sliced

1/4 cup (2 fl oz/60 ml) fruity Italian white wine

1/2 cup (4 fl oz/125 ml) meat or vegetable stock

1/4 cup (2 fl oz/60 ml) heavy (double) cream

salt, pepper, and freshly grated nutmeg to taste

❖ Preheat oven to 425°F (220°C/Gas Mark 6).

❖ For the filling, in a frying pan over medium heat, melt the butter. Add the onion and sauté for 1 minute. Raise heat to medium-high, add the garlic and spinach, and sauté until spinach is wilted, 2–3 minutes. Stir in the sun-dried tomatoes. Transfer the spinach mixture to a colander and, using the back of a wooden spoon, press gently against the mixture to remove any excess moisture, then allow to cool. Wipe the pan clean and set aside.

❖ Transfer the spinach mixture to a bowl and stir in the Parmesan cheese, salt, and pepper.

❖ Place each chicken breast half between plastic wrap and, with the flat side of a meat mallet, pound until ¼ inch (6 mm) thick. Place one cheese slice on top of each pounded breast. Spoon one-fourth of the spinach filling onto the bottom center of each cheese slice and shape the filling into a log, being careful that it does not protrude over the edges. Fold the sides in toward the center and, beginning at the bottom end, roll up tightly. Secure with toothpicks.

❖ In the frying pan over medium-high heat, warm the oil. While the oil is heating, spread the flour on a plate. Roll the stuffed chicken breasts in the flour to coat lightly and evenly. Add chicken to the pan and brown lightly on all sides, 5–7 minutes.

❖ Transfer the chicken to a baking dish. Place in the center of the oven and immediately reduce the heat to 375°F (190°C/Gas Mark 4). Bake until cooked through, 10–12 minutes.

filled breasts in mushroom-wine sauce

✣ For the sauce, in a small frying pan over medium heat, melt the butter. Add the onion and cook until the edges begin to turn translucent, about 2 minutes. Add the mushrooms and cook until barely limp, about 2 minutes. Pour in the wine and deglaze the pan by stirring to dislodge any browned bits from the bottom of the pan. Over medium heat, cook until the wine is reduced by half, about 2 minutes. Add the stock and simmer until reduced by half, 3–4 minutes. Pour in the cream and simmer until the sauce thickens slightly, 1–2 minutes. Add salt, pepper, and nutmeg.

✣ Spoon sauce over chicken and serve immediately.

recipe variations

For a richer, more intense sauce, substitute eggplant (aubergine) for the mushrooms and use a heavy red wine instead of the light fruity one. Chop the eggplant into small cubes and cook it for longer than you would the mushrooms, 5–8 minutes.

chicken provençale

2 cups (8 oz/250 g) cubed peeled eggplant (aubergine)

2 tomatoes, peeled, seeded, and chopped

1 onion, halved and thinly sliced

1 each red and green bell peppers (capsicums), cut into thin strips

¼ cup (2 fl oz/60 ml) red or dry white wine, or chicken stock

2 tablespoons chopped fresh basil

2 cloves garlic, minced

2 teaspoons salt

4 skinless, boneless chicken breast halves (1 lb/500 g total)

1 tablespoon olive oil or vegetable oil

½ teaspoon paprika

◈ In a large saucepan, combine the eggplant, tomatoes, onion, bell peppers, wine or stock, basil, garlic, and salt. Bring to a boil, then reduce heat. Simmer, covered, for 10 minutes. Uncover and simmer until the vegetables are just tender and nearly all of the liquid is evaporated, a further 5 minutes.

◈ Place each breast half between plastic wrap. With the flat side of a meat mallet, pound to ¼ inch (6 mm) thick.

◈ In a large frying pan, heat the oil and paprika over medium-high heat. Add the chicken and cook until cooked through, 4–6 minutes. Serve the vegetables topped with the chicken.

chicken with fresh tomato chutney

serves 4

2 lb (1 kg) chicken thighs, skinned, if desired

1 tablespoon vegetable oil

2 tomatoes, peeled, seeded, and chopped

2 tart cooking apples, chopped

1 jalapeño or other hot chile, seeded and finely chopped

¼ cup (2 oz/60 g) dried currants or raisins

½ red bell pepper (capsicum), chopped

1 small onion, chopped

¼ cup (2 fl oz/60 ml) cider vinegar

1 tablespoon sugar

2 teaspoons peeled and grated fresh ginger

salt to taste

✧ In a large frying pan over medium-high heat, warm the oil. Add the chicken and brown on all sides. Spoon off fat.

✧ In a large mixing bowl, stir together the tomatoes, apples, chile, currants or raisins, bell pepper, onion, vinegar, sugar, ginger, and salt. Add to the pan along with the chicken. Bring to a boil, then reduce heat. Cover and simmer until chicken is cooked through, 35–40 minutes. Remove chicken from pan and keep warm.

✧ Boil chutney mixture, uncovered, until thick, about 5 minutes. Serve with chicken.

cajun chicken with mustard sauce

serves 8

1 cup (4 oz/125 g) all-purpose (plain) flour

2 teaspoons dried oregano, crumbled

2 teaspoons ground cumin

2 teaspoons ground coriander

1 teaspoon ground thyme

½ teaspoon cayenne pepper

salt to taste

⅓ cup (2½ oz/80 g) unsalted butter

4 skinless, boneless chicken breast halves (1 lb/500 g total)

combination of your favorite mustard varieties

◈ In a shallow dish, combine the flour, oregano, cumin, coriander, thyme, cayenne pepper, and salt.

◈ In a small saucepan, melt 3 tablespoons of the butter. Dip each piece of chicken in butter then in the flour mixture.

◈ In a large frying pan over medium heat, melt the remaining butter. Add chicken and sauté until browned and cooked through, 10–15 minutes.

◈ Serve with a dipping sauce made from the mustards.

tangy fried chicken

serves 4

As a special treat, resist the temptation to remove the skin and leave it on this chicken. It crisps up nicely and turns a beautiful brown for an appetizing presentation—and the flavor is delicious.

MARINADE

4 cloves garlic

½ teaspoon salt

⅓ cup (2½ fl oz/80 ml) lime juice

2 tablespoons olive oil or vegetable oil

2 tablespoons water

1 teaspoon ground cumin

¼ teaspoon ground turmeric

pepper to taste

FRIED CHICKEN

2–2½ lb (1–1.8 kg) meaty chicken breasts, thighs, and drumsticks

¼ cup (1 oz/30 g) all-purpose (plain) flour

2 tablespoons olive oil or vegetable oil

◈ Preheat oven to 375°F (190°C/Gas Mark 4).

◈ For the marinade, using a mortar and pestle, mash the garlic with the salt to form a paste. In a small bowl, combine the garlic-salt mixture, lime juice, 2 tablespoons oil, water, cumin, turmeric, and pepper.

◈ For the fried chicken, pour the marinade into a plastic bag. Add the chicken pieces, seal, and turn the bag to coat chicken with the marinade. Marinate in the refrigerator for 8–24 hours, turning the bag occasionally. Drain marinade from chicken and discard marinade. Pat chicken dry with paper towels.

◈ Place the flour in a clean plastic bag. Add chicken, two or three pieces at a time, and shake the bag to coat the chicken with flour. In a large ovenproof frying pan over medium-low heat, warm the 2 tablespoons of oil. Add the chicken and cook, uncovered, for 10–15 minutes, turning to brown evenly. Spoon off fat. Transfer the pan to oven. Bake, uncovered, until the chicken is cooked through, 30–35 minutes.

chicken fajitas

serves 4

¾ lb (375 g) chicken breast meat, cut into 2- x ½-inch (4- x 1-cm) strips

¼ cup (2 fl oz/60 ml) vegetable oil

¼ cup (2 fl oz/60 ml) lime juice

¼ cup (2 fl oz/60 ml) tequila or water

2 tablespoons chopped cilantro (fresh coriander)

2 cloves garlic, minced

1 teaspoon ground cumin

salt and pepper to taste

8 x 7-inch (18-cm) flour tortillas

1 tablespoon vegetable oil

1 onion, halved and thinly sliced

1 green, red, or yellow bell pepper (capsicum), cut into thin strips

½ cup (5 oz/160 g) chopped fresh or canned tomatoes

TO SERVE (OPTIONAL)

guacamole

sour cream

salsa

shredded Cheddar cheese

❖ Preheat oven to 350°F (180°C/Gas Mark 4).

❖ In a plastic bag set in a deep bowl, place chicken strips. To the bag, add the ¼ cup (2 fl oz/ 60 ml) oil, lime juice, tequila or water, half the cilantro, the garlic, cumin, and salt and pepper. Seal the bag and massage gently to combine the marinade ingredients and coat the chicken. Marinate in the refrigerator for 4–24 hours, turning occasionally. Drain chicken from marinade and discard marinade. Set chicken aside.

❖ Wrap the tortillas in aluminum foil and place in the oven for 10 minutes to warm. In a large frying pan over medium-high heat, warm the 1 tablespoon oil. Add onion and cook, stirring, for 12 minutes. Add bell pepper and cook, stirring, until crisp-tender, about 12 minutes further. Remove the vegetables from pan.

❖ To the hot pan, add the chicken and cook, stirring, until cooked through, 2–3 minutes. Return all vegetables to the pan. Add the tomatoes. Cook, stirring, until heated through, 1–2 minutes. Stir in the remaining cilantro.

❖ To serve, fill tortillas with the chicken and vegetable mixture. If desired, top with guacamole, sour cream, salsa, and/or cheese.

serves 6

CHICKEN

*1 cup (5 oz/155 g)
all-purpose (plain) flour*

*1½ teaspoons dried basil,
crushed*

salt and pepper to taste

onion powder

*3–3½-lb (1.5–1.75-kg)
chicken, cut into 6 pieces
(skinned if desired)*

*½ cup (4 fl oz/125 ml)
buttermilk*

2 tablespoons vegetable oil

GRAVY

*2 tablespoons all-purpose
(plain) flour*

*1 teaspoon instant chicken
bouillon granules (stock
powder)*

pepper to taste

1¾ cups (14 fl oz/440 ml) milk

❖ For the chicken, in a heavy-gauge plastic bag, combine the flour, basil, salt and pepper, and onion powder. Add the chicken pieces, two or three at a time, to the plastic bag and shake to coat with the flour mixture. Dip the pieces, one at a time, into the buttermilk. Add again to the plastic bag with the flour mixture, shaking to coat.

❖ In a 12-inch (30-cm) frying pan over medium heat, warm the oil. Add the chicken and cook for 15 minutes, turning to brown evenly. Reduce heat to medium-low and cook, uncovered, turning occasionally, until cooked through, 35–40 minutes. Remove chicken from the pan and drain on paper towels. Transfer to serving dish and keep warm.

❖ For the gravy, stir the flour, bouillon granules, and pepper into the drippings in the frying pan, scraping up any browned bits. Add the milk and cook, stirring, over medium heat until mixture is thick and bubbly. Cook and stir for a further 1 minute. Serve with the chicken pieces.

crispy fried chicken

chicken wings
with barbecue sauce

serves 6

6 cups (1½ qt/1.5 l) vegetable oil, for deep-frying

18 small chicken wings (about 2½ lb/1.25 kg total)

3 tablespoons butter

⅔ cup (5 fl oz/160 ml) hot barbecue sauce

½ cup (4 fl oz/125 ml) sour cream

3 oz (90 g) blue cheese, crumbled

coarsely cracked black pepper to taste

1 green (spring) onion, finely chopped

dash of lemon juice

3 large stalks celery, cut into 2-inch (5-cm) sticks (optional)

In a large saucepan, heat the oil to 365°F (185°C). Deep-fry the chicken wings until golden and crisp, about 15 minutes. Remove and drain.

In a small pan over medium heat, melt the butter. Add the barbecue sauce and stir until smooth. Keep hot.

Combine the sour cream, blue cheese, pepper, green onion, and lemon juice and mix to make a smooth dip. Spoon into a small serving dish.

Pour the barbecue sauce over the chicken, brushing each piece so it is thickly and evenly coated. Place the dip in the center of a wide serving dish and surround with the chicken. If desired, decorate dish with the celery, or serve separately.

119

sautéed chicken
with cranberry glaze

serves 4

4 skinless, boneless chicken breast halves (1 lb/500 g total), each cut into 4 diagonal slices

1 cup (5 oz/155 g) all-purpose (plain) flour, for coating

2 tablespoons vegetable oil

ground black pepper to taste

1 cup (8 fl oz/250 ml) chicken stock

1 cup (8 fl oz/250 ml) port

¼ cup (2¾ oz/80 g) cranberry sauce

⅓ cup (1¾ oz/50 g) fresh or frozen cranberries

❖ Place each chicken slice between plastic wrap. Using the flat side of a meat mallet, lightly pound to a ¼-inch (5-mm) thick oval. Coat with flour, shaking off excess.

❖ Heat the oil in a frying pan over high heat, add half the chicken ovals, sprinkle with pepper, and cook, turning once, until well browned and cooked through, about 2 minutes each side. Remove from pan and keep warm. Repeat with the remaining chicken ovals.

❖ Drain any excess fat from the pan, add the chicken stock and port, and simmer, uncovered, until reduced to about 1 cup (8 fl oz/250 ml). Stir in cranberry sauce and cranberries. Heat until warmed through. Serve immediately with the chicken.

chicken pâté

makes 2 cups (16 oz/500 g)
serves 6 as an appetizer

*3 tablespoons unsalted
butter*

3 tablespoons olive oil

*1 lb (500 g) chicken livers,
trimmed and patted dry*

3 onions, chopped

*½ cup (4 fl oz/125 ml)
dry white wine*

*2 garlic cloves, coarsely
chopped*

1 tablespoon dried sage

*1 tablespoon chopped
fresh rosemary*

ground black pepper to taste

3 tablespoons capers

5 anchovy fillets

2 teaspoons tomato paste

❖ In a heavy-based pan over moderate heat, warm the butter and oil. Add the chicken livers and onions and sauté until browned, about 10 minutes. Add the wine, garlic, sage, rosemary, and pepper and cook until the liquid has reduced, about 3 minutes. Add the capers, anchovies, and tomato paste. Stir well, then cook for a further 1 minute. Cool the mixture.

❖ Transfer mixture to a food processor and process until almost smooth. Transfer to a serving bowl, cover, and refrigerate for at least 2 hours before serving. Serve with crackers, toast, or on fresh crusty bread.

the ultimate
chicken
sandwich

serves 4

2 x 6-oz (170-g) jars artichoke hearts, drained

1 onion, sliced

2 tablespoons chopped fresh basil

½ cup (2 oz/60 g) drained roasted bell peppers (capsicums) in oil, sliced

2 tablespoons oil from roasted bell peppers (capsicums)

7 oz (220 g) fresh asparagus spears

4 skinless, boneless chicken breast halves (1 lb/500 g total)

⅓ cup (3 oz/90 g) butter

1 tablespoon olive oil

ground black pepper to taste

DIJON MAYONNAISE

⅓ cup (3 fl oz/90 ml) mayonnaise

1 tablespoon Dijon mustard

¼ teaspoon Tabasco sauce

salt and pepper to taste

8 slices rye bread, cut ½ inch (1.25 cm) thick

1 bunch (4 oz/120 g) arugula (rocket), washed and stemmed

the ultimate chicken sandwich

❖ Combine the artichoke hearts, onion, basil, bell peppers, and oil in a bowl and toss well.

❖ Boil, steam, or microwave the asparagus until just tender, then drain.

❖ Place each chicken breast half between plastic wrap and, with the flat side of a meat mallet, gently pound until ¼ inch (6 mm) thick. Cut them in half crosswise.

❖ In a large frying pan over high heat, warm 2 tablespoons of the butter and the olive oil. Add the chicken, sprinkle with pepper, and cook until cooked through, about 3 minutes.

❖ For the Dijon mayonnaise, in a bowl, combine the mayonnaise, mustard, Tabasco sauce, and salt and pepper and mix well.

❖ Spread the bread slices with the remaining butter and top half the bread slices with the arugula, chicken, asparagus, artichoke mixture, and Dijon mayonnaise. Top with the remaining bread slices. Serve while still warm.

recipe variations

To add a touch of the exotic to this recipe, fry some ginger, garlic, and chile (to taste) in the olive oil and butter before adding the chicken. Also, toss in a handful of cilantro (fresh coriander) before removing the chicken. Use a simple balsamic vinegar and olive oil dressing instead of the mayonnaise.

sherry chicken

1/4 cup (1 oz/30 g)
all-purpose (plain) flour

salt and pepper to taste

4 skinless, boneless chicken
breast halves (1 lb/500 g total)

2 tablespoons olive oil or
vegetable oil

1 clove garlic, cut into
thin slivers

1/2 cup (4 fl oz/125 ml)
cream sherry

1 cup (8 fl oz/250 ml)
orange juice

2 tablespoons orange
marmalade

1/4 cup (2 oz/60 g) sliced
(flaked) almonds, toasted

hot cooked rice

❖ In a large plastic bag, combine the flour and salt and pepper. Add the chicken, one piece at a time, shaking the bag to coat chicken with flour mixture.

❖ In a frying pan over medium heat, warm the oil. Add the chicken and cook until cooked through, turning once, 10–15 minutes total. Transfer chicken to a serving dish and keep warm.

❖ In the same pan, in the pan drippings, add the garlic. Cook, stirring, for 15 seconds. Carefully add the sherry and bring to a boil. Boil gently, uncovered, until reduced by half, 1–2 minutes. Stir in the orange juice and marmalade and bring to a boil. Boil gently, uncovered, until slightly thickened, 2–3 minutes. Pour over the warm chicken and sprinkle with the toasted almonds. Serve with rice.

chicken sandwich with olives

serves 4

1/4 cup (2 oz/60 g) chopped pimiento-stuffed olives or Kalamata olives

1 small tomato, chopped

1 tablespoon chopped fresh parsley

2 teaspoons drained capers (optional)

1/2 teaspoon dried Italian seasoning, crushed

1 teaspoon olive oil or vegetable oil

4 skinless, boneless chicken breast halves (1 lb/500 g total)

2 tablespoons olive oil or vegetable oil

4 lettuce leaves

4 slices sourdough bread, toasted

❖ In a small mixing bowl, stir together the olives, tomato, parsley, capers (if using), Italian seasoning, and the 1 teaspoon oil. Set aside.

❖ Place each breast half between plastic wrap and pound lightly with the flat side of a meat mallet to a 1/4-inch (6-mm) thickness.

❖ In a large frying pan, over medium-high heat, warm the 2 tablespoons of oil. Add the chicken and cook until cooked through, turning once, 4–6 minutes total. Remove from pan. To serve, place the lettuce leaves on toasted sourdough bread. Top with the chicken breasts and olive mixture.

rhineland burgers

serves 4

serves 4

1 egg, beaten

2 tablespoons milk

¼ cup (1 oz/30 g) fine dry
bread crumbs

2 green (spring) onions,
finely chopped

2 tablespoons chopped
fresh parsley

1 teaspoon anchovy paste

1 teaspoon finely shredded
lemon zest

salt and pepper to taste

1 lb (500 g) ground (minced)
chicken

2 tablespoons margarine or butter

toasted bread or hamburger buns

❖ In a mixing bowl, stir together the egg, milk, bread crumbs, green onion, parsley, anchovy paste, lemon zest, and salt and pepper. Add the chicken and mix well. (The mixture will be soft.) Shape the chicken mixture into four ¾-inch (2-cm) thick patties.

❖ In a large frying pan over medium heat, melt the margarine or butter. Add the patties and cook until cooked through, turning once, 8–12 minutes total.

❖ Serve atop bread or hamburger buns.

mozzarella and prosciutto rolls

serves 4

The combination of
mozzarella cheese and
prosciutto, two typically
Italian ingredients, gives this
dish an unmistakably Italian
flavor. It is a simple yet
elegant dish with which to
create a great impression.

4 skinless, boneless chicken
breast halves (1 lb/500 g total)

salt and pepper to taste

1 tablespoon tomato paste

1 cup (4 oz/125 g) shredded mozzarella cheese

4 large, paper-thin slices prosciutto

very small pinch dried thyme (optional)

1½ cups (6 oz/185 g) all-purpose (plain) flour

2 eggs, beaten

1½ cups (6 oz/185 g) fine dry bread crumbs

vegetable oil or a mixture of oil and butter,
for pan frying

✧ Place the breast halves between plastic wrap and, using the flat side of a meat mallet, pound them to a ¼-inch (5-mm) thickness. Sprinkle with salt and pepper and spread the tomato paste over the inside of each breast. Sprinkle mozzarella cheese over half of each piece and lay the prosciutto on top, folding in layers. Sprinkle on the thyme, if using. Fold the pieces in half and pinch around the edges to enclose the filling.

✧ In three separate shallow dishes, put the flour, beaten eggs, and bread crumbs. Dip the chicken into the flour, coating thinly and evenly, then dip into the egg and allow to drain before placing in the bread crumbs. Place on a plate, cover with plastic wrap, and refrigerate for 1–2 hours.

✧ In a large frying pan over medium heat, warm the oil. Fry the chicken rolls until golden brown on the surface and just cooked through, turning once, about 5 minutes. Serve at once with pasta and vegetables.

recipe hint

The chicken rolls can be prepared several hours in advance, or the night before. Cover and refrigerate until ready to use.

stir-frying

stir-frying basics

Like sautéing, stir-frying is a quick-cooking method in an open pan using only a little fat. The main difference is that sautéing is a classic French cooking method that usually involves larger pieces of meat cooked in a straight-sided frying pan, whereas stir-frying is an Asian technique that requires all the ingredients to be small and of uniform size. These are tossed in a hot wok (a pan with flared sides and usually a round bottom).

Stir-frying is extremely fast and cooking time is often a matter of seconds, not minutes—and certainly never hours! There is no time to stop between steps to prepare more ingredients or mix a sauce—the cooking happens very quickly. While the food is cooking, it is constantly stirred. This method is a healthful way to prepare food, as the brief cooking times produce meat that is juicy and flavorsome and crisp-tender vegetables full of nutrition.

Preparation for stir-frying is vital. Before you begin, it is essential that you measure, mix, cut up, and slice all ingredients. Have them in bowls or plates next to you, within a hand's reach, while cooking. Remember, you won't have time to do any preparation once you begin to cook.

It is also important to have the right equipment. If you do not have a wok, make sure you have a large, heavy-based frying pan that will not burn your food over high heat. Woks are designed specifically for stir-frying because they evenly distribute heat and the flared sides allow you to separate ingredients while cooking. This allows for control over cooking times and temperatures.

stir-frying basics

There are many types of wok, so buy the one that you feel most comfortable with and that suits the type of stove you have. There are flat-bottomed woks for use on electric stovetops and round-bottomed woks for gas stovetops. There are also non-stick and electric woks. Woks are available from most kitchenware stores and from Asian markets and supermarkets. (If you do buy a wok, remember you can also use it to deep-fry, steam, and braise food.)

Another vital piece of equipment for stir-frying is a wok spatula or a long-handled wooden spoon. The spatula is ideal because it allows you to take up a good quantity of the cooking food and turn it to cook evenly. Although the ideal equipment for stir-frying is a wok and a wok spatula, generally you can make do with a large frying pan and a long-handled wooden spoon.

When preparing to stir-fry, make sure you cut each type of food into same-size pieces. For instance, if you are cutting meat, cut all the pieces to the same size. Other ingredients such as vegetables may be cut larger or smaller than the meat, or than each other, but each type of vegetable should be cut into pieces of uniform size. This ensures equal cooking time and takes away the worry that some pieces will be undercooked while others may be burnt.

Stir-fried vegetables are often bias-sliced. To bias-slice, simply hold a knife at a 45-degree angle to the vegetable and make a diagonal cut, then make evenly spaced cuts the entire length of the vegetable. Long vegetables, such as carrots, beans, and celery are perfect for bias-slicing.

When you begin stir-frying, make sure the wok is hot. Pour the oil around the top of the wok, letting it flow down the sides. Swirl it around to coat the entire inside of the wok. Always begin with food that takes the longest time to cook, then add foods that are quicker to cook.

thai-style
chicken and spinach

serves 4

¼ cup (2 fl oz/60 ml)
chicken stock

1 tablespoon Thai fish sauce
or 2 teaspoons soy sauce

1 tablespoon cornstarch
(cornflour)

2 tablespoons chopped
cilantro (fresh coriander)

12 oz (375 g) chicken thigh meat,
cut into 1-inch (2.5-cm) pieces

1 tablespoon hot chile oil, or
1 tablespoon sesame oil with
¼ teaspoon chile powder added

1¼ lb (625 g) spinach leaves,
washed and trimmed

3 cloves garlic, minced

3 tablespoons chopped peanuts

◈ In a small bowl, combine the stock, fish sauce or soy sauce, and cornstarch. Mix well.

◈ In a large mixing bowl, toss the cilantro with the chicken. In a wok over medium-high heat, warm the oil. Add the chicken and stir-fry until cooked through, 2–3 minutes. Remove the chicken from the wok.

◈ Add the spinach and garlic to the wok and toss to mix. Add the chicken and reduce heat to medium-low. Cover and cook for 3 minutes. Push the chicken and vegetables to the sides of the wok.

◈ Stir the chicken stock mixture. Add to the center of the wok and cook, stirring, until thick and bubbly. Stir all ingredients together to coat with the sauce, and cook for a further 1 minute. Spoon into a serving dish and sprinkle with the peanuts just before serving.

pepper
chicken
chiuchow-style

serves 4–6

MARINADE

1 teaspoon salt

1 teaspoon sugar

1 teaspoon rice wine

2 teaspoons cornstarch (cornflour)

1 tablespoon water

CHICKEN

8 oz (250 g) chicken breast meat, cut into
¾-inch (2-cm) cubes

2 cups (16 fl oz/500 ml) groundnut
(peanut) oil

12 fresh chin jiu leaves (see note, page 137)
or mint leaves

½ teaspoon ground Sichuan peppercorns

black pepper to taste

2 teaspoons salted fish sauce

1 teaspoon dark soy sauce

1 teaspoon rice wine

2 tablespoons chicken stock

For the marinade, in a medium bowl, combine the salt, sugar, rice wine, cornstarch, and water. Mix well. Add the chicken and coat with the marinade. Cover and marinate for 15 minutes.

In a wok or large frying pan over medium heat, warm the oil. Add the mint leaves and fry until crisp. Remove the mint leaves from the wok and drain them on paper towels.

To the wok, over medium heat, add the chicken and fry until it turns white, about 45 seconds. Remove the chicken from the wok and drain on paper towels.

Drain all but 1–2 tablespoons of the oil from the wok and warm over high heat. Add the chicken, the Sichuan peppercorns, black pepper, fish sauce, soy sauce, rice wine, and stock. Stir-fry until most of the liquid has evaporated, about 4 minutes. Place on a serving dish and garnish with the mint leaves. Serve immediately while hot.

recipe hint

You will probably need to use mint leaves for this recipe, as *chin jiu* leaves are difficult to find outside Asia. *Chin jiu* means "pearl leaf." The taste is not important, because the leaves soak up much of the oil—it is their melt-in-the-mouth texture for which they are valued. If you cannot find them under their Chinese name, try in Thai markets and ask for *bai horaphaa*. Mint leaves are a good substitute, as the minty taste disappears when they are deep-fried.

sichuan
chicken with peanuts

serves 4–6

MARINADE

1 tablespoon light soy sauce

1 teaspoon dark soy sauce

1 teaspoon sugar

1 teaspoon rice wine

2 teaspoons cornstarch (cornflour)

CHICKEN

1½ lb (750 g) chicken breast meat,
cut into ½-inch (12-mm) cubes

1 cup (8 fl oz/250 ml) groundnut
(peanut) oil

1 red chile, seeded and chopped

2 dried red chiles, chopped

2 garlic cloves, crushed

1 tablespoon hot fava (broad) bean paste

1 teaspoon sugar

1 teaspoon Sichuan peppercorns, ground

⅓ cup (3 fl oz/100 ml) chicken stock

2 green (spring) onions, cut into
1-inch (2.5-cm) lengths

2–3 tablespoons roasted ground peanuts

1 teaspoon rice wine

⬨ For the marinade, in a medium bowl, combine the soy sauces, sugar, rice wine, and cornstarch. Mix well. Add the chicken and coat with the marinade. Cover and marinate for 30 minutes.

⬨ In a wok or frying pan over medium-high heat, warm the oil. Add the chicken and fry until it turns white, about 45 seconds. Remove the chicken from the wok and drain on paper towels.

⬨ Drain all but 1–2 tablespoons of oil from the wok and warm over high heat. Add the chile, dried chiles, and garlic and stir-fry for 30 seconds. Add the bean paste, sugar, and peppercorns. Stir to mix.

⬨ Return the chicken to the wok and stir-fry for about 30 seconds. Add the stock and cook, stirring, for about 30 seconds further. Add the green onions, peanuts, and rice wine. Stir well and serve.

recipe variations

To give this dish a bit more of a bite, add 1 extra fresh chile and 1 extra dried chile. Or, if you are looking for a milder dish, omit the chiles completely and add 1 tablespoon of oyster sauce in place of the bean paste. You could also add straw mushrooms at the end of cooking—cover and simmer for 2 minutes before serving.

chicken
with straw mushrooms

MARINADE

1 tablespoon light soy sauce

1 teaspoon dark soy sauce

1 teaspoon sugar

CHICKEN

1½ lb (750 g) chicken breast meat,
cut into finger-size strips

1 cup (8 fl oz/250 ml)
groundnut (peanut) oil

3–4 slices peeled fresh ginger

12 dried straw mushrooms, soaked in warm
water for 1 hour to soften, drained

1 cup (8 oz/250 g) cauliflower florets,
blanched

2 spring (green) onions,
cut into 1-inch (2.5-cm) lengths

1½ teaspoons salt

1 teaspoon sugar

½ cup (4 fl oz/125 ml) chicken stock

1 teaspoon rice wine

◈ For the marinade, in a medium bowl, combine the soy sauces and sugar. Mix well. Add chicken and coat with the marinade. Cover and marinate for 30 minutes.

◈ In a wok or large frying pan over high heat, warm the oil. Add the chicken and stir-fry until it turns white, about 45 seconds. Remove the chicken from the wok and drain on paper towels.

◈ Drain all but 1–2 tablespoons oil from the wok and warm over high heat. Add the ginger and mushrooms and stir-fry for 30 seconds. Add the cauliflower and stir.

◈ Return the chicken to the wok and stir-fry for a further 30 seconds. Add the green onions, salt, sugar, and stock. Stir well. Add the rice wine and serve.

food fact

The secret of this dish is in the mushrooms. Straw mushrooms are raised in northern Guangdong province, China, and are among the most fragrant of all mushrooms. The fragrance is further enhanced when they are dried, because a special chemical reaction occurs that makes them even tastier. These mushrooms are available in any Chinese grocery shop.

honey ginger chicken

serves 4–6

CHICKEN MARINADE

1 tablespoon light soy sauce

1 teaspoon dark soy sauce

1 teaspoon rice wine

1 teaspoon salt

1 tablespoon cornstarch (cornflour)

1 lb (500 g) chicken legs, chopped into bite-size pieces

GINGER MARINADE

1 tablespoon sugar

1 teaspoon salt

1 tablespoon white vinegar

4 oz (125 g) young ginger, chopped into bite-size pieces and lightly crushed

2 cups (16 fl oz/500 ml) groundnut (peanut) oil

1 red and 1 green bell pepper (capsicum), cut into small squares

1 tablespoon honey

1 teaspoon dark soy sauce

1 teaspoon salt

1 teaspoon rice wine

1 cup (8 fl oz/250 ml) chicken stock

For the chicken marinade, in a small bowl, combine the soy sauces, rice wine, salt, and cornstarch. Mix well. Add the chicken and coat with the marinade. Cover and marinate for 30 minutes.

For the ginger marinade, in a small bowl, combine the sugar, salt, and vinegar. Add the ginger and coat in the marinade. Marinate for 30 minutes.

In a wok over medium-high heat, warm the oil. Add the ginger and fry until lightly browned. Remove the ginger from the wok and drain on paper towels.

Add the chicken to the wok and fry until it turns white, about 45 seconds. Remove the chicken from the wok and drain on paper towels.

Drain all but 2–3 tablespoons of the oil from the wok and warm over high heat. Add the bell peppers and stir-fry for 30 seconds. Add the chicken and ginger to the wok. Reduce the heat to medium-low. Add the honey, soy sauce, salt, rice wine, and stock, cover, and cook for 3 minutes. Serve immediately.

food fact

This dish is best made with freshly marinated young ginger, which is far superior to commercially pickled ginger. The pickling takes only half an hour and doing it yourself makes all the difference. Young ginger is recognizable by its pale, thin skin (it doesn't need peeling) and its ivory color. It also tastes lighter and fresher than mature ginger.

asian pan-fried noodles

serves 4

salt to taste

1 lb (500 g) fresh thin Chinese egg noodles

peanut (groundnut) oil, for pan-frying

SAUCE

1 tablespoon cornstarch (cornflour)

1 cup (8 fl oz/250 ml) chicken stock

1/2 teaspoon sugar

pepper to taste

1 1/2 tablespoons soy sauce

1 1/2 teaspoons oyster sauce

TOPPING

3/4 lb (375 g) chicken breast meat, cut into 1/2-inch (12-mm) cubes

1 teaspoon peeled and minced fresh ginger

1 teaspoon minced garlic

6 green (spring) onions, cut into 2-inch (5-cm) lengths

salt to taste

1/4 lb (125 g) large shrimp (king prawns), peeled and deveined

1 small red bell pepper (capsicum), cut into 1 1/2-inch (4-cm) squares

1/4 lb (125 g) fresh shiitake mushrooms, stemmed and sliced

3/4 lb (375 g) baby bok choy, cut into 2-inch (5-cm) lengths

1 teaspoon sesame oil

❖ Fill a large pot three-fourths full of water and bring to a boil. Salt lightly. Gently pull the noodles apart and add to the pot, stirring to separate the strands. Bring to a boil again and cook for 1 minute. Pour the noodles into a colander and rinse them thoroughly with cold water. Drain well and toss with 1 tablespoon peanut oil to keep the strands from sticking together.

❖ Preheat oven to 250°F (120°C/Gas Mark 1). Put a baking sheet in the oven.

❖ In a frying pan over medium-high heat, warm ½ tablespoon of the oil. Add one-fourth of the noodles. Using a wide spatula, spread them evenly over the bottom of the pan to form a pancake. Reduce heat to medium. Cook until the bottom is golden brown, 4–5 minutes. Using the spatula, turn the noodle pancake over and brown the other side, about 3 minutes further. Add more oil, if needed, to prevent scorching. Transfer pancake to the baking sheet to keep warm. Repeat to make four noodle pancakes in total.

❖ For the sauce, in a small bowl, combine the cornstarch, stock, sugar, pepper, soy sauce, and oyster sauce. Stir to make a smooth paste.

❖ For the topping, in a wok over medium-high heat, warm 1 tablespoon of peanut oil. Add the ginger, garlic, green onions, and salt and cook until fragrant, about 15 seconds. Increase heat to high. Add the chicken and shrimp and stir-fry until the chicken turns white and the shrimp are pink, about 1½ minutes. Transfer the mixture to a bowl.

asian pan-fried noodles

❖ Add the bell pepper, mushrooms, and bok choy to the wok. Stir-fry over medium-high heat until the mushrooms begin to shrink, about 3 minutes. Add more peanut oil, if needed, to prevent sticking. Stir the sauce. Add to the wok and bring to a boil. Stir continuously until the sauce is glossy and thick, about 30 seconds. Return chicken-shrimp mixture to the wok and add 1 teaspoon sesame oil. Toss together to mix.

❖ Divide the noodle pancakes among four serving plates and evenly distribute the topping over each cake. Serve immediately.

food fact

Bok choy is a common Asian vegetable with long, white stalks with dark green leaves, a mild, chardlike flavor, and a crunchy texture. It is also known as pak choi, Chinese white cabbage, or mustard cabbage. Baby bok choy is about half the size and more tender. Select bunches whose leaves and stalks are crisp, firm, and brightly colored. Avoid those that have brown spots, bruising, or cracked or wilted leaves. Refrigerate in a plastic bag for up to 4 days. Before using, trim the stalks to remove the tough ends. If using leaves only, separate the leaves from the stalks and chop or shred as desired.

fried rice

serves 4

4 shallots or 1 yellow onion, coarsely chopped

2 cloves garlic, peeled

1 teaspoon dried shrimp paste

2 small red chiles, seeded

1/2 teaspoon ground turmeric

2 tablespoons tomato ketchup

1 tablespoon sweet dark soy sauce

2 tablespoons light soy sauce

3 tablespoons peanut or corn oil, plus extra if needed

5 cups (25 oz/780 g) cold, cooked white rice

1 1/2 cups (4 1/2 oz/140 g) shredded green cabbage

3/4 cup (4 oz/125 g) green peas, blanched and drained

1/4 lb (125 g) shrimp (prawns), peeled and deveined

1 cup (6 oz/185 g) diced, cooked chicken

4 green (spring) onions, sliced

4 eggs

OPTIONAL GARNISHES

fried shallot flakes (page 149)

fried shrimp crackers (page 149)

fried rice

✤ Using a mortar and pestle or mini food processor, grind or process the shallots or onion, garlic, shrimp paste, chiles, and turmeric to a paste.

✤ In a small bowl, combine the ketchup and soy sauces. Mix well.

✤ In a wok over medium-high heat, warm 2 tablespoons of the oil. Add the spice paste and stir-fry until fragrant, about 2 minutes.

✤ Increase heat to high. Using your palms, crumble the cold rice into the wok. Using a wok spatula, toss and gently flatten any clumps of rice until the grains are separated. Add the ketchup mixture and stir-fry until all rice grains are evenly coated. Add the cabbage, peas, shrimp, and chicken and stir-fry until the shrimp turns pink, 2–3 minutes. Divide among four serving plates and garnish with the green onions. Cover loosely to keep warm.

✤ In a wok over medium-high heat, warm ½ tablespoon of oil. When the oil is almost smoking, crack 1 egg directly into the wok. Fry until the edges are blistered and crisp and the whites are almost set, about 1 minute. Using a slotted spatula, turn the egg over and fry just until brown, a few seconds more. Place the fried egg atop one plate of fried rice. Repeat with the remaining oil and eggs. If desired, sprinkle with fried shallots and garnish with shrimp crackers. Serve hot.

fried shallot or garlic flakes

8 shallots or garlic cloves, cut crosswise into slices 1/8 inch (3 mm) thick

peanut or vegetable oil for frying

In a large frying pan over medium heat, pour in peanut or vegetable oil to a depth of 1/2 inch (12 mm). When the oil is moderately hot (about 325°F/165°C), add the shallot or garlic slices. Fry them slowly, stirring, just until golden brown, 2–3 minutes. Using a slotted spoon, transfer the slices to paper towels and drain. Let cool before serving. (Flakes can be stored in an airtight container at room temperature for up to several weeks.)

Makes about 1/2 cup (1 1/2 oz/45 g)

fried shrimp crackers

These "crackers" or "chips," made from shrimp, fish, or melingo nuts, are popular Asian garnishes. They are primarily made in Indonesia, where they are called *krupuk*. The crackers are dehydrated and look like hard, dry chips. When they are deep-fried, they expand greatly and puff up. They may be served hot, warm, or cold.

To deep-fry shrimp crackers, in a wok or large saucepan over medium heat, pour in groundnut (peanut) oil to a depth of about 2 inches (5 cm). When the oil is hot (about 375°F/190°C), drop in a few crackers. Fry only a few at a time to give them plenty of room to expand. As soon as they puff, in just a few seconds, use long chopsticks or tongs to turn them over and fry on the other side for a few seconds. Immediately transfer the fried crackers to paper towels to drain. Let them cool a little before serving.

sichuan chicken
noodles

serves 5 as a main course

3 tablespoons light soy sauce

2 tablespoons rice vinegar or white wine vinegar

1 teaspoon chile oil, or 1 teaspoon sesame oil with 1/8 teaspoon chile powder added

1/4–1/2 teaspoon crushed chile flakes

5 oz (155 g) dried or 8 oz (250 g) fresh Chinese egg noodles

3 qt (3 l) water

1 tablespoon vegetable oil, plus extra as needed

2 cloves garlic, minced

6 oz (185 g) fresh snow peas (mangetouts), coarsely chopped

1 large red or green bell pepper (capsicum), cut into thin strips

2 green (spring) onions, sliced

1 lb (500 g) chicken breast meat, cut into 3/4-inch (2-cm) pieces

1 1/2 oz (45 g) coarsely chopped peanuts

In a small bowl, combine the soy sauce, vinegar, chile oil, and chile flakes. Stir well.

If using dried noodles, bring a large saucepan containing the water to a boil. Add noodles, reduce heat slightly, and boil, uncovered, stirring occasionally, until tender, 4–6 minutes. If using fresh noodles, prepare according to package directions. Drain noodles.

In a wok or large frying pan over medium-high heat, warm the vegetable oil. (Add more oil as needed during cooking.) Add the garlic and stir-fry until flavors release, 15 seconds. Add the snow peas, bell pepper, and green onions and stir-fry until crisp-tender, 1–2 minutes. Remove the vegetables from the wok.

Add half the chicken to the wok and stir-fry until cooked through, 2–3 minutes. Remove the chicken from the wok. Stir-fry the remaining chicken in the same way, then return the first batch of cooked chicken to the wok. Add the soy sauce mixture, cooked vegetables, and noodles. Stir together to coat with the soy sauce mixture. Cook, stirring, until heated through, about 1 minute further. Sprinkle with the peanuts and serve immediately.

sweet and sour
crispy
noodles

serves 6–8 as an appetizer

1/2 lb (250 g) crispy fried rice sticks
(page 153)

juice and zest of 1 lime

1 tablespoon yellow bean paste

2 tablespoons tomato paste

2 tablespoons Thai fish sauce

1/4 cup (2 oz/60 g)
firmly packed brown sugar

2 tablespoons peanut or corn oil

3/4 lb (375 g) chicken breast meat,
cut into 1/4-inch (6-mm) thick slices

1/4 lb (125 g) shrimp (prawns), peeled
and deveined

2 cloves garlic, chopped

4 shallots, chopped

1 tablespoon dried small shrimp (optional)

2 small red chiles, thinly sliced on the
diagonal

OPTIONAL GARNISHES

3 cups (6 oz/185 g) bean sprouts

1 lime, cut into wedges

cilantro (fresh coriander) leaves

✧ Prepare the rice sticks (see right).

✧ In a small bowl, combine the lime juice, bean sauce, tomato paste, fish sauce, and sugar. Mix well.

✧ In a wok or large frying pan over medium-high heat, warm the oil. Add the chicken and shrimp and stir-fry until they feel firm to the touch, about 1 minute. Remove the chicken and shrimp from the wok.

✧ Add to the wok the garlic, shallots, and dried shrimp (if using). Stir-fry until fragrant, 30 seconds. Raise heat to high. Add the lime juice mixture and stir-fry until it is glossy and syrup-like, 2 minutes more.

✧ Reduce heat to medium. Gently fold in the crispy noodles and the chiles—try not to crush the noodles. Mix in the reserved shrimp mixture and the lime zest. Transfer to a platter, piling the mixture into a mound. Pile the bean sprouts and lime wedges, if using, at one end of the platter. Top with the cilantro, if desired. Serve immediately.

crispy fried rice sticks

Rice stick noodles come in 1-lb (500-g) packages, often separated into four wafers. Holding one wafer inside a paper bag to capture any shreds, break it apart into several small portions.

In a wok or saucepan over medium heat, pour in peanut oil to 2 inches (5 cm). When hot (about 375°F/190°C), drop in noodles, one portion at a time. When they puff, a few seconds, turn them over with long chopsticks or tongs and fry on the other side for a few seconds. Immediately transfer to paper towels to drain. Cool, then store in an airtight container at room temperature for up to 4 days.

mongolian chicken

serves 4

MARINADE

2 teaspoons groundnut (peanut) oil

salt to taste

1/4 teaspoon sugar

2 teaspoons cornstarch (cornflour)

10 oz (300 g) chicken breast meat, bias-cut into 1/4-inch (5-mm) x 2-inch (5-cm) slices

1/2 teaspoon minced garlic

2 teaspoons freshly ground chiles

1/2 teaspoon finely chopped onion

2 teaspoons ground bean sauce (mo si jeung) (available at Chinese stores)

2 teaspoons cold water

2 teaspoons sugar

1 tablespoon groundnut (peanut) oil

1 tablespoon rice wine or dry sherry

1/3 cup (3 fl oz/90 ml) chicken stock

1 teaspoon dark soy sauce

4 dried Chinese mushrooms (available at Chinese stores), soaked in warm water for 45 minutes, rinsed, water squeezed out, stems discarded, and caps halved

1/2 small red bell pepper (capsicum), cut into 1-inch (2.5-cm) triangles

3 green (spring) onions, mainly white parts, cut into 2-inch (5-cm) lengths

1/2 teaspoon cornstarch (cornflour), mixed with 2 teaspoons cold water

1 teaspoon sesame oil

For the marinade, in a medium bowl, combine the oil, salt, sugar, and cornstarch. Mix well. Add the chicken and coat with marinade. Cover and marinate while you prepare the other ingredients.

In a small bowl, combine the garlic, chiles, and onion. Mix well. In a separate small bowl, combine the bean sauce, water, and sugar. Mix well.

In a wok over medium-high heat, warm the oil. Add the garlic mixture and stir-fry for about 5 seconds. Add the bean sauce mixture and stir-fry for a further 5 seconds. Add the rice wine or sherry. Stir well. Add the stock and soy sauce. Stir well. Increase the heat to high. Add the chicken, mushrooms, bell pepper, and green onions and stir-fry for 2–3 minutes further. Reduce heat a little.

Add the cornstarch mixture. Stir until the sauce is slightly thickened, a few seconds, then add the sesame oil. Stir and serve hot.

recipe **hint**

When cooking garlic, always take care not to burn it, or it will take on a bitter taste. In this recipe, once you add the garlic, chile, and onion to the wok, stir constantly. Also, don't leave garlic in the wok for too long. These steps will ensure that it does not burn.

chicken
cantonese

serves 4

MARINADE

2 tablespoons soy sauce

1 tablespoon rice wine or chicken stock

2 teaspoons cornstarch (cornflour)

12 oz (375 g) chicken breast meat,
cut into thin bite-size strips

1 cup (8 fl oz/250 ml) chicken stock

1 tablespoon cornstarch (cornflour)

5 oz (155 g) dried or 8 oz (250 g) fresh
Chinese egg noodles

3 qt (3 l) water

1 teaspoon toasted sesame oil

1 tablespoon vegetable oil, plus extra as
needed

2 cloves garlic, minced

2 teaspoons peeled and grated fresh ginger

1 carrot, thinly bias-sliced

1/2 cup (4 oz/125 g) thinly bias-sliced celery

1 red or green bell pepper (capsicum), cut
into 1- x 1 1/4-inch (2.5- x 3-cm) slices

1/2 cup (4 oz/125 g) chopped onion

1 cup (3 oz/90 g) sliced fresh mushrooms

1/3 cup (2 oz/60 g) coarsely chopped
almonds

✦ For the marinade, in a medium mixing bowl, combine the soy sauce, rice wine or stock, and the 2 teaspoons cornstarch. Mix well. Add the chicken and coat with the marinade. Cover and marinate for 30 minutes. Do not drain.

✦ In a small bowl, combine the stock and the 1 tablespoon of cornstarch. Mix well.

✦ If using dried noodles, bring a large saucepan containing the water to a boil. Add noodles, reduce heat slightly, and boil, uncovered, stirring occasionally, until tender, 4–6 minutes. If using fresh noodles, prepare according to package directions. Drain noodles and stir in the sesame oil. Keep warm.

✦ In a wok or large frying pan over medium-high heat, warm the vegetable oil. (Add more oil as needed during cooking.) Add the garlic and ginger and stir-fry for 15 seconds. Add the carrot and stir-fry for a further 1 minute. Add the celery and stir-fry for a further 1 minute. Add the bell pepper and onion and stir-fry for a further 1 minute. Add the mushrooms and stir-fry until vegetables are crisp-tender, a further 1 minute. Remove the vegetables from the wok.

✦ Add the almonds to the wok and stir-fry until roasted, 2–3 minutes. Remove the almonds from the wok. Add the undrained chicken and stir-fry until cooked through, 3–4 minutes. Push the chicken to the edges of the wok. Stir the stock-cornstarch mixture. Add to the center of the wok and cook, stirring, until thick and bubbly. Return the vegetables and almonds to the wok. Stir all ingredients together to coat with the sauce. Cook, stirring, until heated through, about 1 minute further. Serve tossed through the noodles.

crystal chicken with broccoli

serves 4

BATTER

4 oz (125 g) all-purpose (plain) flour

¼ teaspoon baking powder

6 fl oz (180 ml) water

2 teaspoons soy sauce

2 cloves garlic, flattened

12 oz (375 g) chicken breast meat, cut into bite-size strips

3 fl oz (90 ml) honey

2 teaspoons soy sauce, extra

2 tablespoons cider vinegar

2 tablespoons light molasses (golden syrup)

2 tablespoons water

2 tablespoons dry sherry

2 cloves garlic, minced

2 teaspoons cornstarch (cornflour)

oil for deep-frying

1 tablespoon vegetable oil, plus extra as needed

3 cups (10 oz/315 g) broccoli florets

❖ For the batter, in a small mixing bowl, combine the flour, baking powder, 6 fl oz (180 ml) water, 2 tablespoons soy sauce, and flattened garlic. Mix well. Let stand for 15 minutes. Remove and discard garlic. Add the chicken to the batter. Stir gently to coat.

❖ In a small mixing bowl, combine the honey, extra soy sauce, vinegar, molasses, remaining water, sherry, garlic, and cornstarch. Mix well. Set aside.

❖ In a wok or 2-quart (2-l) saucepan over medium heat, pour 2 inches (5 cm) of oil and heat to 365°F (185°C). Remove chicken from the batter and allow excess to drain off. Fry chicken strips, a few at a time, until golden, 30–60 seconds per batch. Drain on paper towels.

❖ In a large frying pan over medium heat, warm the 1 tablespoon of vegetable oil. (Add more oil as needed during cooking.) Add the broccoli and stir-fry until crisp-tender, 4–5 minutes. Remove broccoli from the pan and arrange it around the edge of a serving platter. Keep warm.

❖ Stir the honey-soy mixture. Add to the pan and cook, stirring, until thick and bubbly. Cook, stirring, for a further 1 minute. Return the chicken to the pan and heat through. Pour the chicken and sauce into the center of the broccoli-lined serving platter. Serve immediately.

serves 4

MARINADE

1/3 cup (3 fl oz/90 ml) hoisin sauce

2 cloves garlic, crushed

2 tablespoons dry sherry

1 tablespoon honey

2 tablespoons soy sauce

1/4 teaspoon five-spice powder

*1 lb (500 g) chicken breast meat,
thinly sliced*

*1 lb (500 g) package
fresh thick egg noodles*

2 tablespoons vegetable oil

1 onion, sliced lengthwise

2 cloves garlic, crushed

*4 bunches (10 oz/300 g)
bok choy, washed*

*1/2 each red, green, and yellow bell
peppers (capsicums), thinly sliced*

2 tablespoons cold water

*1 tablespoon cornstarch
(cornflour)*

❖ In a dish, combine marinade ingredients and chicken and mix well. Cover and refrigerate for several hours or overnight. Drain the chicken, reserving the marinade.

❖ Add the noodles to a pan of boiling water, simmer, uncovered, for 3 minutes, then drain.

❖ In a wok or large frying pan over high heat, warm the oil. When hot, add a few of the chicken pieces and cook, stirring, until the chicken is browned and cooked through. Remove from wok and set aside. Repeat in batches with the remaining chicken pieces.

❖ Reheat the wok over medium heat, add the onions and garlic, and cook, stirring, until the onion is soft. Add the bok choy and bell peppers and cook, stirring, until the bok choy is wilted. Add the noodles, toss well, and transfer to serving plates.

❖ Blend the reserved marinade with the cornstarch and water. Add to the wok and cook, stirring, until the mixture boils and thickens. Return the chicken to the wok and stir-fry until heated through. Spoon onto the bok choy mixture on the serving plates.

hoisin
noodle stir-fry

ginger chicken
with mushrooms

serves 4

1 cup (6 oz/180 g) small snow peas (mangetouts),
tips and strings removed

1 cup (5 oz/155 g) loose-pack frozen peas

¾ cup (6 fl oz/180 ml) half-and-half (half cream)
or light cream

2 teaspoons cornstarch (cornflour)

salt and pepper to taste

1 tablespoon vegetable oil

2 teaspoons peeled and grated fresh ginger

2½ cups (8 oz/250 g) fresh shiitake
mushrooms or other mushrooms,
stems removed, caps sliced

12 oz (375 g) chicken breast meat,
cut into thin bite-sized strips

¼ cup (¼ oz/10 g) chopped
fresh Italian (flatleaf) parsley

❖ In a medium pan over medium heat, boil all peas until snow peas are crisp-tender, about 1 minute. Drain and set aside.

❖ In a bowl, stir together half-and-half or light cream, cornstarch, salt, and pepper. Set aside.

❖ In a wok or large frying pan over medium-high heat, warm the oil. (Add more oil as necessary during cooking.) Stir-fry the ginger for 30 seconds. Add the mushrooms and stir-fry until tender, about 2 minutes. Remove the vegetables from the wok.

❖ Add the chicken strips to the hot wok. Stir-fry until cooked through, 3–4 minutes. Push chicken to edges of wok. Stir the half-and-half mixture and pour into the center of the wok. Cook, stirring, until the mixture is thick and bubbly. Return the vegetables to the wok. Stir all ingredients together to coat with the sauce. Cook, stirring, until heated through, a further 1 minute. Sprinkle with the parsley and serve immediately.

stir-fried chicken
and asparagus

serves 4

1 egg white, lightly beaten

1 tablespoon cornstarch
(cornflour)

1 tablespoon dry white wine

1 clove garlic, minced

salt and pepper to taste

1 lb (500 g) chicken thigh meat,
cut into thin, bite-size strips

2 tablespoons chile sauce

2 tablespoons soy sauce

1 tablespoon wine vinegar

1–1½ teaspoons chile oil

1 tablespoon vegetable oil

1 lb (500 g) fresh asparagus
spears, bias-sliced into
2-inch (5-cm) pieces

1 red bell pepper (capsicum),
cut into bite-size strips

4 green (spring) onions,
bias-sliced into 1-inch
(2.5-cm) pieces

❖ In a medium mixing bowl, stir together
the egg white, cornstarch, wine, garlic, and
salt and pepper. Stir in the chicken strips.
Cover and let stand at room temperature
for 20–30 minutes. Do not drain.

❖ Meanwhile, in a small mixing bowl, stir
together the chile sauce, soy sauce, wine
vinegar, and chile oil. Set aside.

❖ In a wok or large frying pan over
medium heat, warm the vegetable oil. Add
half of each of the asparagus, bell pepper,
and green onions and stir-fry until crisp-
tender, 3–4 minutes. Remove from the wok.
Repeat with the remaining vegetables.

❖ Add the undrained chicken strips to
the hot wok. Stir-fry until cooked through,
3–4 minutes. Return the cooked vegetables
to the wok. Stir chile sauce mixture and mix
into the chicken and vegetables. Cover and
cook until heated through, about 1 minute.
Divide among warmed bowls and serve.

spaghettini
with tomato-basil sauce

serves 4

2 tablespoons olive oil

5 oz (155 g) prosciutto, sliced

4 skinless, boneless chicken breast halves
(1 lb/500 g total), sliced into thick strips

1 tablespoon balsamic vinegar

1 lb (500 g) dried spaghettini

1 tablespoon extra-virgin olive oil

2 cloves garlic, crushed

6 large tomatoes (about 3 lb/1.5 kg),
peeled and finely chopped

1/3 cup (1/3 oz/10 g) chopped fresh basil

5 oz (150 g) bocconcini, cubed

1 cup (4 oz/125 g) grated Parmesan cheese

2 teaspoons sugar

1/4 cup (1 oz/30 g) drained, oil-packed,
sun-dried tomatoes, sliced

salt and pepper to taste

❖ In a large frying pan over medium-high heat, warm the 2 tablespoons olive oil. Add the prosciutto, cook until just crisp, then drain. Reheat pan, add the chicken, and stir-fry until cooked through. Add the balsamic vinegar and stir until chicken is well coated.

❖ Bring a large pan of salted water to a boil. Add the spaghettini and boil until just tender, 10–12 minutes or as directed on package. Drain; keep warm.

❖ In a medium frying pan over medium heat, warm the extra-virgin olive oil. Add the garlic, tomatoes, and basil and bring to a boil. Reduce the heat and simmer, uncovered, until the mixture is pulpy, about 10 minutes. Stir in the bocconcini and half the Parmesan, the sugar, sun-dried tomatoes, and salt and pepper. Toss through the spaghettini.

❖ Top the spaghettini with the chicken, prosciutto, and remaining Parmesan.

167

stir-fried thai noodles

serves 4

½ lb (250 g) dried flat rice stick noodles, ¼ inch (6 mm) wide

1 oz (30 g) tamarind pulp, coarsely chopped

½ cup (4 fl oz/125 ml) boiling water

2½ tablespoons vegetable oil, or as needed

8 large fresh shrimp (prawns), peeled, deveined, and cut in half lengthwise

1 skinless, boneless whole chicken breast (about 4 oz/125 g), cut crosswise into slices ¼ inch (6 mm) thick

1½ teaspoons dried small shrimp (prawns) (optional)

2 tablespoons chopped preserved radish (optional)

1 tablespoon chopped garlic

3 tablespoons Thai fish sauce

3 tablespoons fresh lime juice

2 tablespoons sugar

3 eggs

4 green (spring) onions, cut into 1½-inch (4-cm) lengths

1½ cups (3 oz/90 g) bean sprouts

¼ teaspoon red pepper flakes

cilantro (fresh coriander) leaves for garnish

2 tablespoons chopped dry-roasted peanuts

1 lime, cut into wedges

stir-fried thai noodles

Although this dish is traditionally made with flat rice stick noodles, thin dried rice vermicelli can also be used. Dried shrimp and preserved radishes can be difficult to find (try Asian markets), but they provide considerable flavor and texture, making them well worth the search.

❖ In a large bowl, combine the rice stick noodles with warm water to cover. Let stand until soft and pliable, about 20 minutes. Drain and set aside.

❖ Meanwhile, in a small bowl, soak the tamarind pulp in the boiling water for 15 minutes. Mash with the back of a fork to help dissolve the pulp. Pour through a fine-mesh sieve into another small bowl, pressing against the pulp to extract as much liquid as possible. Discard the pulp and set the liquid aside.

❖ Preheat a nonstick wok over medium-high heat. Add 1 tablespoon of the oil. When the oil is hot, add the shrimp and chicken and stir-fry until the shrimp turn pink and chicken turns white, about 1½ minutes. Transfer to a plate and set aside.

❖ Add the remaining 1½ tablespoons oil to the wok over medium-high heat. Add the dried shrimp, radish (if using), and the garlic. Stir-fry until the garlic turns light brown, about 30 seconds. Add the tamarind liquid, fish sauce, lime juice, and sugar. Increase heat to high and cook, stirring, until well mixed and almost syrupy, about 1 minute.

❖ Crack the eggs directly into the sauce and gently scramble them just until the yolks are broken up. Cook until the eggs begin to set, 1–2 minutes, then gently fold them into the sauce. Add the green onions, 1 cup (2 oz/60 g) of the bean sprouts, the red pepper flakes, and the drained noodles. Toss gently until the sprouts begin to wilt, about 1 minute.

❖ Return the shrimp-chicken mixture to the wok and stir-fry until the noodles begin to stick together, 2–3 minutes. Transfer to a serving dish and top with the remaining ½ cup (1 oz/30 g) bean sprouts. Garnish with the cilantro leaves and peanuts. Serve with lime wedges.

recipe variations

Vary the fresh shellfish you use in this recipe. Instead of the shrimp (prawns), try a combination of shrimp and scallops or shrimp and baby squid. You can also vary the ratio of chicken to seafood to give quite a different flavor to this dish.

sesame
chicken and vegetables

serves 6

SAUCE

½ cup (4 fl oz/125 ml) chicken stock

2 tablespoons soy sauce

1 tablespoon sesame oil

4 cloves garlic, minced

2–3 teaspoons peeled and grated
fresh ginger

2 teaspoons cornstarch (cornflour)

1 teaspoon sugar

CHICKEN

½ cup (2 oz/60 g) all-purpose (plain) flour

2 tablespoons sesame seeds

salt and chile powder to taste

1 egg, lightly beaten

¼ cup (2 fl oz/60 ml) milk

vegetable oil for deep-frying

1 lb (500 g) skinless, boneless chicken
thighs, cut into ¾-inch (2-cm) pieces

VEGETABLES

1 tablespoon vegetable oil, plus extra
as needed

2 zucchinis (courgettes), cut into thin,
bite-size strips

1 green bell pepper (capsicum), cut into
thin, bite-size strips

6 green (spring) onions, bias-sliced into
½-inch (12-mm) pieces

For the sauce, in a small bowl, combine the stock, soy sauce, sesame oil, garlic, ginger, cornstarch, and sugar. Mix well.

Preheat oven to 300°F (150°C/Gas Mark 2).

For the chicken, in the bowl of an electric mixer, combine the flour, sesame seeds, and salt and chile powder. Stir to combine. In a small mixing bowl, combine the egg and milk. Mix well and add to the dry ingredients. Using the electric mixer, mix until smooth.

In a wok or 2-qt (2-l) saucepan over medium heat, pour in 1¼ inches (3 cm) vegetable oil. Heat to 365°F (185°C). Dip the chicken, one piece at a time, into the coating, then slip each piece carefully into the hot oil. Fry the chicken, a few pieces at a time, until golden, about 4 minutes for each batch. Using a slotted spoon, remove the chicken. Drain on paper towels. Place on a baking sheet in the oven to keep warm while you fry the remaining chicken pieces.

For the vegetables, in a large frying pan over medium-high heat, warm the oil. (Add more oil as needed during cooking.) Add the zucchini, bell pepper, and green onions and stir-fry until crisp-tender, 3 minutes. Push the vegetables to the edges of the pan. Stir the sauce, add to the pan, and cook, stirring, until thick and bubbly. Then cook for a further 1 minute.

Add the cooked chicken to the pan. Stir all ingredients together to coat with the sauce. Serve immediately.

sweet and sour
chicken

1 x 1-lb (500-g) can pineapple chunks (juice pack)

¼ cup (2 fl oz/60 ml) tomato ketchup

2 tablespoons cornstarch (cornflour)

2 tablespoons red wine vinegar

2 tablespoons water

4 teaspoons sugar

1 egg, lightly beaten

12 oz (375 g) skinless, boneless chicken breast meat, cut into 1-inch (2.5-cm) cubes

¾ cup (2 oz/60 g) finely crushed crackers (savory biscuits)

1 tablespoon vegetable oil, plus extra as needed

1 green and 1 red bell pepper (capsicum), cut into ½-inch (12-mm) pieces

4 green (spring) onions, bias-sliced into 1½-inch (4-cm) pieces

hot cooked rice (optional)

❖ Preheat oven to 300°F (150°C/Gas Mark 2).

❖ Drain the pineapple and reserve ¾ cup (6 fl oz/190 ml) of the juice. In a small bowl, stir together the pineapple juice, ketchup, 1 tablespoon cornstarch, the vinegar, water, and sugar.

❖ In a mixing bowl, combine the egg and remaining 1 tablespoon cornstarch. Stir until smooth. Add the chicken pieces and stir to coat the chicken with the egg mixture. Place the cracker crumbs in a shallow dish. Roll the chicken pieces in the cracker crumbs to coat evenly.

❖ In a wok or large frying pan over medium-high heat, warm the oil. (Add more oil as needed during cooking.) Add half the chicken and stir-fry until cooked through, about 3 minutes. Remove the chicken and transfer to the oven to keep warm. Repeat with the remaining chicken.

❖ Add the bell peppers and green onions to the wok and stir-fry until crisp-tender, 2–3 minutes. Remove the vegetables from the wok.

❖ Stir the pineapple juice mixture. Add to the wok and cook, stirring, until thick and bubbly. Then cook, stirring, for a further 2 minutes. Return the chicken and vegetables to the wok. Add the pineapple chunks. Stir all ingredients together to coat with the sauce. Cook, stirring, until heated through, about 1 minute further. Serve with rice, if using.

microwaving

microwaving basics

Microwave ovens are easy to use, quick, clean, and safe—and they won't heat up your kitchen. In just 20 minutes you can have a beautifully cooked chicken dish, or precooked chicken pieces ready to use in salads, soups, casseroles, or however you wish.

If you have never used a microwave oven, here is some background information that you may find useful. A conventional oven uses currents of hot, dry air to cook food, whereas a microwave oven uses short, high-frequency radio waves to bombard the food. These waves only penetrate about 1 inch (2.5 cm) into the food (depending on the density) and cause the moisture inside the food to vibrate and generate heat. Microwave cooking is extremely quick, but because it is so fast, food can progress in an instant from cooked and juicy to dry and overdone. Also, it is easy to cook food unevenly if it is not turned and/or stirred during cooking.

To use a microwave oven effectively, you need microwave-safe dishes. They must be glass, ceramic, or plastic (never metal or metal trimmed). Some dishes made of these materials may not be microwave-safe, but most manufacturers' labels will tell you if they are not. If you are unsure, try this test: fill a glass measuring cup with water and place the cup and the baking dish in the microwave. Cook on high (100%) for 1 minute. If the dish stays cool, then it is probably safe to use. If it gets hot, then don't use it. (The glass of water is merely to prevent damage to the oven, as microwave ovens should not be operated when empty.)

microwaving basics

When a recipe calls for covered cooking, use a well-fitting lid or tightly cover the dish with plastic wrap. This stops any steam escaping and allows the food to cook quickly and evenly.

When you are cooking chicken pieces, arrange them in a single layer in a microwave-safe dish. Arrange the pieces skin-side up with the meatiest parts facing the edges of the dish. To keep the splashes from the cooking chicken off the microwave oven's walls, loosely cover the dish with kitchen towel or waxed paper. Halfway through cooking, using tongs, turn the pieces of chicken over and rearrange them so the less-cooked parts are nearer the edges of the dish.

When cooking a whole chicken, it is recommended that you begin cooking with the chicken breast-side down and turn it once, halfway through cooking. Make sure you cover the wing tips and the ends of the legs with aluminum foil to prevent further cooking and drying out. Basting will add flavor and color to the chicken.

With chicken, it is vital that you do not undercook, to avoid salmonella contamination. To test a whole chicken for doneness, grasp the end of a drumstick—if it easily moves up and down and twists in its socket, it is done. Before carving, check that the juices run clear.

NOTE: Microwave ovens operate on varying wattages. Cooking times in this book are based on a 650-watt microwave oven. If you are using an oven of a different wattage, then make cooking time adjustments as follows: *For every 1 minute of cooking time* add or subtract the following number of seconds for the wattage of your microwave oven: 700 watt (subtract 5 seconds); 600 watt (add 5 seconds); 550 watt (add 10 seconds); 500 watt (add 20 seconds); 450 watt (add 30 seconds); and 400 watt (add 40 seconds).

chicken and camembert mousse

1 cup (4 oz/125 g)
Camembert cheese

½ cup (4 fl oz/125 ml) mayonnaise

1 cup (8 fl oz/250 ml)
natural yogurt

3 tablespoons chopped fresh chives

1 teaspoon Dijon mustard

1 teaspoon dried mixed herbs

3 teaspoons gelatin

⅓ cup (3 fl oz/90 ml)
chicken stock

2 cups (8 oz/250 g) chicken breast
meat, cooked and ground (minced)

❖ Using a food processor, process the cheese, mayonnaise, yogurt, chives, mustard, and mixed herbs. (Or, shred the cheese, then, using a fork, beat the mayonnaise, yogurt, chives, mustard, and mixed herbs until smooth, then add the cheese.)

❖ In a small microwave-safe bowl, combine the gelatin and stock. Stir well. Cook on high (100%) until warm, 1 minute. Stir until gelatin dissolves. Stir the gelatin-stock mixture into the cheese mixture. Gently fold in the chicken.

❖ Pour the mixture into a wetted 2-cup (16-fl oz/500-ml) mold. Chill overnight to allow the flavors to develop. Serve cold with fresh bread or toast.

paella

serves 4–6

3 oz (90 g) shrimp (prawns), shelled and deveined

3 oz (90 g) mussels, shelled

3 oz (90 g) white fish fillets, roughly chopped

1 tablespoon butter

2 tablespoons olive oil

1 onion, chopped

13 oz (410 g) chicken breast meat, cut into bite-size pieces

1 tomato, peeled and chopped

1 green bell pepper (capsicum), sliced

1 clove garlic, crushed

pinch of paprika

1 teaspoon powdered saffron, or to taste

1½ cups (8 oz/250 g) long-grain rice

2 cups (16 fl oz/500 ml) boiling water

1 cup (5 oz/155 g) frozen peas

3 oz (90 g) calamari, cut into rings

3–4 cooked spicy sausages

In a shallow microwave-safe dish, place the shrimp, mussels, and fish. Dot with the butter. Cover and cook on high (100%) until the fish is cooked through, about 3–4 minutes. Set aside.

In a 3-qt (3-l) microwave-safe dish or casserole, mix together the oil and onion. Cover and cook on high until the onion is tender, 2 minutes. Add the chicken, cover, and cook for a further 3 minutes. Stir in the tomato, bell pepper, garlic, and paprika. Cover and cook on high for 5 minutes. Add the saffron, rice, boiling water, peas, and calamari. Stir well. Cook, uncovered, on medium (50%) until all the water is absorbed and the rice is cooked, 15–20 minutes.

Add the shrimp, mussels, fish, and cooked sausages. Carefully stir. Cook on medium until heated through, 2–3 minutes. Transfer paella to a serving dish and serve while still hot.

recipe variations

Paella, a classic Spanish dish, is a mixture of seafood, chicken, and sometimes rabbit or snails. Some or all of these ingredients may be omitted, or replaced with vegetables of your choice. Potatoes, sweet potatoes, and pumpkin, cut into large roasting-size pieces, will take about as long to cook as the shrimp, mussels, and fish. Instead of the calamari, you could use broccoli florets. If using frozen peas, there is no need to thaw them first.

roast chicken dinner

serves 4

This wonderfully
simple recipe for a
"roast" dinner takes
just over 35 minutes!

1 whole chicken, 3 lb (1.5 kg)

2 tablespoons butter, melted

4–6 (655 g–1 kg) potatoes, peeled and quartered

11 oz (345 g) asparagus spears, trimmed

1 lb (500 g) broccoli, cut into small florets

$1/3$ cup ($2^1/2$ fl oz/80 ml) boiling water

2 teaspoons cornstarch (cornflour)

◈ Tie the chicken legs to tail, skewer neck skin to back, and twist the wings under the back. Brush the whole chicken with the melted butter.

◈ Place the chicken, breast-side down, on a microwave roasting rack or upturned saucer, set in a microwave-safe dish. Cook on high (100%) for 8 minutes. Turn the chicken over and cover the wing tips and ends of legs with aluminum foil. Cook on high for a further 4 minutes. Baste with the pan juices. Cook on high until cooked through, a further 5–8 minutes. Remove the chicken from the dish. Cover with aluminum foil and allow to stand for 15 minutes. Drain the juices from the dish. Reserve and set aside to allow fat to rise to surface. Skim off and discard the fat from the surface.

◈ At one end of a large, shallow, microwave-safe dish, place the potatoes. Cover and cook on high for 8 minutes. Turn the potatoes over and put the cooked ones toward the center. Carefully place the asparagus in the center of the dish and the broccoli at the other end from the potatoes. Cover and cook on high until broccoli and asparagus are crisp-tender, about 3 minutes more. Remove the dish from the microwave and allow to stand for 5 minutes. If desired, in a medium frying pan over high heat, sauté the potatoes until browned, 1–2 minutes.

◈ In a small microwave-safe bowl, add the reserved juices, boiling water, and the cornstarch. Blend with a little cold water. Cook on high until bubbling and thick, 3–5 minutes, stirring after every 1 minute. Strain into a gravy boat, if necessary.

◈ Serve the chicken on a serving platter with the vegetables.

honey-baked chicken

serves 4–5

The honey, butter, and lemon juice mixture in this recipe forms a wonderful glaze for the chicken, imbuing it with a delicious tangy-sweet taste. The honey also gives it a wonderful golden color.

2 sprigs fresh parsley

1 sprig fresh thyme

2 sprigs celery tops

1 bay leaf

1 whole chicken, about 3 lb (1.5 kg)

1/3 cup (4 oz/125 g) honey

1 teaspoon butter

1 teaspoon lemon juice

salt and ground black pepper to taste

❖ Using kitchen string, tie together the parsley, thyme, celery tops, and bay leaf. Place in the body cavity of the chicken. Tie the chicken legs to tail, skewer neck skin to back, and twist the wings under the back. Place the chicken on a roasting rack in a shallow microwave-safe dish.

❖ In a small microwave-safe dish, combine the honey, butter, lemon juice, and salt and pepper. Mix well. Cook on high (100%) until blended, about 2 minutes, stirring after 1 minute. Brush some of the glaze over the chicken. Place the chicken, breast-side down, on a microwave roasting rack or upturned saucer, set in a microwave-safe dish. Cover the wing tips and ends of legs with aluminum foil. Cook on high for 4 minutes. Reduce power to medium high (70%) and cook for a further 15–18 minutes. Remove foil, turn chicken breast-side up, and brush with the honey glaze. Cook on medium high until cooked through, 15–18 minutes more, brushing with glaze several times during cooking. Transfer the chicken to a heated serving dish and brush once more with the glaze. Cover loosely with aluminum foil and let stand in a warm place for 10–12 minutes before carving and serving.

chicken marengo

4 drumsticks and 4 whole thigh
pieces (about 2 lb/1 kg total)

1 teaspoon all-purpose
(plain) flour

1 tablespoon butter

1 large tomato, chopped

½ cup (4 fl oz/125 ml) dry
white wine

1 teaspoon tomato paste

1 teaspoon chicken stock
powder

1 clove garlic, crushed

½ cup (4 fl oz/125 ml) water

1½ cups (5 oz/155 g) sliced
button mushrooms

chopped fresh parsley to taste

❖ Lightly coat the chicken pieces in the flour.

❖ In a medium frying pan over medium heat, melt the butter. Add the chicken pieces and fry until brown, about 2 minutes. Turn chicken pieces over and cook for a further 2 minutes. Transfer to a 6-cup (1½-qt/1.5-l) microwave-safe dish. Add the tomato.

❖ In a small mixing bowl, combine the wine, tomato paste, stock powder, garlic, and water. Mix well. Pour mixture over the chicken. Cover and cook on high (100%) for 5 minutes, stirring well after 3 minutes.

❖ Add the mushrooms and parsley. Cover and cook until chicken is cooked through and the mushrooms are tender, 2 minutes more. Transfer to a serving platter and serve immediately.

chicken paprika

serves 6–8

1 tablespoon butter

1 tablespoon vegetable oil

1 large onion, chopped

1 clove garlic, crushed

2 teaspoons paprika,
or to taste

1 cup (4 fl oz/250 ml)
hot chicken stock

4 lb (2 kg) skinless
chicken pieces

1 teaspoon all-purpose
(plain) flour

½ cup (4 fl oz/125 ml)
sour cream

◈ In a medium microwave-safe casserole, combine the butter, oil, onion, garlic, and paprika. Mix well. Cook on high (100%) until onion is transparent and begins to color slightly, 1 minute. Add the stock and chicken. Mix well. Cook on high for 6–8 minutes, rearranging the chicken after 4 minutes. Reduce to medium high (70%) and cook until chicken is cooked through, 10 minutes, rearranging the chicken after 5 minutes.

◈ In a small bowl, mix together the flour and sour cream. Slowly stir into the casserole dish, mixing well. Cook on medium high for 1–2 minutes more.

◈ Serve with noodles or pasta, if desired.

chicken and asparagus mornay

serves 4

To serve six people, use six chicken pieces and increase the sauce by using 1½ cups (12 fl oz/375 ml) of condensed chicken soup. Cook the chicken for 4–6 minutes, then cook the completed dish on high (100%) for 4 minutes. Complete the cooking time as in the method opposite.

4 skinless, boneless chicken breast halves (1 lb/500 g total), cut in half

lemon pepper to taste

1 tablespoon butter or vegetable oil

1½ tablespoons all-purpose (plain) flour

1 teaspoon mustard

1 cup (8 fl oz/250 ml) canned condensed chicken soup

¾ cup (6 fl oz/180 ml) milk

1 tablespoon mayonnaise

2 tablespoons chopped fresh parsley

black pepper, to taste

10 oz (315 g) asparagus spears

2 cups (10 oz/315 g) long-grain rice

3 tablespoons chopped fresh parsley

2 oz (60 g) cheese-flavored corn chips, crushed

◈ Place the chicken pieces in a large, shallow microwave-safe dish. Sprinkle with lemon pepper. Cover and cook on high (100%) for 4 minutes, turning the chicken pieces over after 2 minutes. Drain the juices from the dish and reserve.

◈ In a 1-qt (1-liter) microwave-safe dish or jug, cook the butter or oil on high for 45 seconds. Stir in the flour and mustard and cook on high for 30 seconds, stirring once. Add the reserved cooking juices from the chicken. Stir well until the mixture forms a thick, smooth sauce. Cook on high for 1 minute. Add the chicken soup, milk, mayonnaise, parsley, and pepper. Stir well.

◈ Add the asparagus to the dish, then the chicken. Pour the sauce over the chicken.

◈ On the stovetop over medium heat, bring a large saucepan of water to boil. Add the rice and cook until tender, 10–15 minutes. Drain. Add the parsley and stir through the rice.

◈ Sprinkle the corn chips on top of the sauce and chicken. Cook on high for 2 minutes. Reduce power to medium high (70%) and cook for a further 2 minutes. Reduce power to medium (50%) and cook for a further 8–10 minutes, or until the asparagus is tender and the chicken is cooked through.

◈ Transfer the hot parsley rice to a serving platter and top with the chicken, sauce, and corn chips. Serve immediately while hot.

oregano chicken with green beans and tagliatelle

serves 4

Oregano and tomato is a combination familiar to most pizza eaters and lovers of Italian food. It is used in this recipe to give a delightfully pungent and robust flavor to the chicken and tagliatelle.

1 tablespoon butter

1 large onion, sliced

2 lb (1 kg) chicken pieces

1 teaspoon all-purpose (plain) flour, seasoned with salt and pepper to taste

14 oz (440 g) canned tomatoes, with juice

½ cup (4 fl oz/125 ml) chicken stock

2 teaspoons dried oregano

1 tablespoon tomato paste

black pepper to taste

1 green bell pepper (capsicum), thinly sliced

8 oz (250 g) dried tagliatelle

1 lb (500 g) green beans, trimmed

✧ In a 3-qt (3-l) microwave-safe dish or casserole, melt the butter on high (100%) for 1 minute. Add the onion and cook on high for 2 minutes.

✧ Toss the chicken in the seasoned flour and add to the onions. Quickly toss to coat the chicken in the melted butter. Cover and cook on high for 5 minutes. Add the tomatoes and their juice, the stock, oregano, tomato paste, black pepper, and bell pepper. Stir well. Cook, uncovered, on high for a further 5 minutes. Cover and cook on medium (50%) until the chicken is cooked through, 12–15 minutes more.

✧ On the stovetop over medium heat, bring a large saucepan of water to a boil. Add the tagliatelle and cook until tender, 10–12 minutes.

✧ In a small, shallow microwave-safe dish, add the green beans. Cover and cook on high until tender, 6–8 minutes.

✧ Drain the tagliatelle and place on a large, warmed serving platter. Top with the chicken. Pass the beans separately.

chicken rosé

1¼ lb (625 g) skinless chicken
pieces

2 teaspoons all-purpose (plain)
flour, seasoned with black
pepper to taste

1 small onion, finely chopped

2 teaspoons vegetable oil

1 clove garlic, crushed

1 green bell pepper (capsicum),
cut into 1-inch (2.5-cm) dice

1 cup (3 oz/90 g) button
mushrooms, quartered

½ cup (2 oz/60 g) canned
tomatoes

¼ cup (2 fl oz/60 ml) rosé wine

¼ teaspoon dried thyme leaves

❖ Coat the chicken pieces in the seasoned flour.

❖ In a shallow, microwave-safe dish, combine the
onion, oil, and garlic. Mix well. Cook on medium high
(70%) for 2 minutes. Add chicken and bell pepper and
cook on medium high for 5 minutes more. Stir well.
Add mushrooms, tomatoes, wine, and thyme. Cover
and cook on medium high for 20 minutes, stirring
occasionally during cooking. Uncover and cook on
medium high until the chicken is cooked through,
about 5 minutes.

❖ NOTE These chicken pieces will yield approximately
8 oz (250 g) cooked meat. To serve four, double the
recipe quantities and cook chicken on medium high for
10 minutes before adding the mushrooms, tomatoes,
wine, and thyme.

chicken
à l'orange

serves 4

finely chopped zest and juice of 1 orange

1 teaspoon raw sugar

1 teaspoon mustard

1 teaspoon stock powder

2 lb (1 kg) skinless, boneless chicken thighs

3 teaspoons cornstarch (cornflour)

1 tablespoon cold water

◈ Combine orange zest and juice, sugar, mustard, and stock powder. Preheat a microwave-safe browning dish on high (100%) for 6 minutes. Toss the chicken in the dish until the sizzling stops and the chicken is browned.

◈ Pour the orange mixture over the chicken. Cover and cook on high for 15 minutes, turning the chicken over and basting with juices after 5 and 10 minutes.

◈ Transfer the chicken to a warmed serving plate. Cover with aluminum foil. In a small bowl, mix the cornstarch with the water to form a paste. Stir into the orange sauce in the cooking dish. Cook until the sauce thickens, 3–4 minutes, stirring after 2 minutes.

◈ Pour the orange sauce over the chicken and serve.

chicken satay

serves 4

MARINADE

1 teaspoon caraway seeds

1 teaspoon ground coriander

1 clove garlic, crushed

1 tablespoon brown sugar

1 tablespoon soy sauce

1 tablespoon lemon juice

1¼ lb (625 g) chicken breast meat, cut into 1-inch (2.5-cm) pieces

SATAY SAUCE

3 red chiles (or to taste), seeded and finely chopped

2 cloves garlic, crushed

1 teaspoon peeled and grated fresh ginger

¼ cup (2 oz/60 g) peanut butter

1 cup (8 fl oz/250 ml) water

¼ cup (1½ oz/45 g) golden raisins (sultanas)

¼ cup (1 oz/30 g) raisins

½ cup (4 fl oz/125 ml) vinegar

½ cup (4 fl oz/125 g) sugar

½ cup (3 oz/90 g) peanuts

1 tablespoon fruit chutney

1 tablespoon vegetable oil

For the marinade, in a large mixing bowl combine the caraway seeds, coriander, garlic, brown sugar, soy sauce, and lemon juice. Add the chicken and mix to coat. Cover and refrigerate for at least 1 hour.

For the sauce, in a 1-qt (1-liter) microwave-safe jug, combine the chiles, garlic, ginger, peanut butter, water, golden raisins, raisins, vinegar, sugar, peanuts, and chutney. Mix well. Cook on high (100%) for 10–12 minutes, stirring halfway through cooking time. Transfer the mixture to a food processor and process until smooth. (Or, push mixture through a fine sieve.)

Preheat a microwave-safe browning dish on high for 7 minutes. Thread chicken cubes onto wooden skewers. Quickly add the oil to the hot browning dish and swirl to coat. Add the chicken pieces and cook on high for 2 minutes. Turn the chicken over and cook on high for a further 3 minutes. (It may be necessary to cook in batches.)

Serve the chicken hot, with the satay sauce either spooned over it or served separately. (To reheat sauce, cook on high for 1–2 minutes. Stir well before serving.)

wings with thai peanut sauce

serves 4

2 teaspoons vegetable oil

4 green (spring) onions,
including green tops, sliced

1 tablespoon Thai curry paste

2 lb (1 kg) chicken wings

1 cup (8 fl oz/250 ml)
coconut milk

1/3 cup (3 oz/90 g) crunchy
peanut butter

1 tablespoon lime or lemon juice

1 tablespoon brown sugar

hot cooked rice, to serve
(optional)

❖ In a large, shallow microwave-safe dish, heat the oil on high (100%) for 30 seconds. Add the spring onions and curry paste. Cook on high for 2 minutes. Add the chicken wings. Stir to coat the chicken with the curry mixture. Cook on high for 3–4 minutes. Add coconut milk, peanut butter, lime or lemon juice, and sugar. Stir. Reduce power to medium high (70%) and cook until chicken is cooked through, a further 15–20 minutes, stirring regularly and adding a little water if the sauce becomes too thick.

❖ Serve chicken and sauce spooned over on a bed of hot cooked rice, if desired.

microwave chicken suprême

4 skinless, boneless chicken
breast halves (1 lb/500 g total),
cut in half

½ cup (4 fl oz/125 ml)
chicken stock

1 tablespoon butter

1 tablespoon all-purpose
(plain) flour

⅔ cup (5 fl oz/160 ml) milk

pinch of mustard powder

white pepper to taste

1 teaspoon lemon juice

2 egg yolks

fresh tarragon leaves
for garnish

In a shallow microwave-safe casserole, combine the chicken and stock. Cover and cook on medium (50%) until the chicken is cooked through, about 5 minutes, turning the chicken halfway through cooking. Transfer to a serving plate. Pour the pan juices into a small measuring jug and add enough water to make up to ⅔ cup (5 fl oz/160 ml).

In a shallow microwave-safe dish, cook the butter on high (100%) for 30 seconds. Add the flour and stir. Cook on high for 30 seconds more. Add the pan juices, milk, mustard powder, pepper, and lemon juice. Cook on high for 5–6 minutes, stirring every minute until the sauce thickens. Add egg yolks and whisk to combine.

Serve chicken and sauce topped with fresh tarragon.

grilling *and* broiling

grilling and broiling basics

Grilling and broiling (known respectively as barbecuing and grilling in Europe, Australia, and New Zealand) are basic cooking methods that are well suited to chicken. They are both based on the same technique, that is, they utilize dry, radiant heat that hits the surface of the food and then travels through to its center. The main difference between broiling and grilling is that broiling is usually done indoors, using the oven, with the heat coming from above the food. Grilling is usually done outdoors and the heat comes from below the food. The aim of both methods is to produce food that is nicely browned on the outside and juicy and tender on the inside.

Tools necessary for broiling and grilling are a cooking rack—one that fits in a broiler pan or sits over the heat of a grill. You will also need long tongs to allow you to turn the food without burning your hands, and a long-handled basting brush. Also, as a general rule, when broiling, the broiler rack should be unheated, whereas for grilling, the grill rack should be heated.

The key to successful broiling is to have the broiler rack and pan at the correct distance from the heat. As a general rule, larger pieces of chicken need more distance from the heat, 5–6 inches (13–15 cm), than do smaller pieces, which need to be about 4 inches (10 cm) from the heat. Also, because broiling doesn't impart a flavor of its own, as grilling can, some seasoning is usually needed to take the blandness out of the chicken. Added flavor can be

grilling and broiling basics

obtained from marinades or bastes. These can also help tenderize the chicken before cooking and help stop it from drying out as it cooks.

When grilling, to ascertain the heat of the grill, hold your hand, palm-side down, at about the height at which food will cook—that is, where the grilling rack will go. If you must pull your hand away after two seconds, the coals are hot; 3 seconds, medium-hot, 4 seconds, medium; 5 seconds, medium-low; and 6 seconds, low.

How you arrange and cut the chicken is also important when broiling or grilling. If broiling, begin cooking with the skin-side down—it is the opposite for grilling, which begins with the skin-side up. Make sure you broil the chicken completely on its underside before basting. For larger pieces of chicken, you don't need to turn the chicken as often as for smaller pieces.

If you are using a marinade that contains raw meat juices, make sure you cook it thoroughly on the meat after you have brushed it on—at least 5 minutes after the last brushing. Or boil the marinade for 2–3 minutes; it may then be brushed onto the chicken up to the last moment.

You can also broil or grill a whole chicken. You will need to "butterfly," or flatten, the bird first. To do this, using poultry or kitchen shears, cut closely along both sides of the backbone for the entire length of the chicken. Discard the backbone. Turn the chicken skin-side up and open it out as flat as possible. Cover with plastic wrap. Strike the breast firmly in the center with the flat side of a meat mallet. (This breaks the breastbone so the bird lies flat.) Twist the wing tips under the back. Halfway between the legs and the breastbone, near the tip of the breast, cut a 1-inch (2.5-cm) slit through the skin on either side of and parallel to the breastbone. Insert the drumstick tips into the slits—this prevents them from popping up during cooking. The chicken is now ready to be broiled or grilled.

honey-glazed
drumsticks

serves 4

GLAZE

1/4 cup (3 oz/90 g) honey

2 tablespoons soy sauce

1 tablespoon cider vinegar

1 tablespoon light molasses
(golden syrup) (optional)

8 chicken drumsticks
(about 2 1/4 lb/1.1 kg total), skin
removed if desired

✤ For the glaze, in a small saucepan, combine the honey, soy sauce, vinegar, and molasses (if using). Mix well. Cook over medium-low heat, stirring occasionally, until bubbling, about 5 minutes.

✤ Turn on broiler (griller). Place the drumsticks on a rack in the broiler pan. Broil (grill), 5–6 inches (13–15 cm) from heat, until the chicken is light brown, about 15 minutes. Turn the chicken and broil until cooked through, a further 10–15 minutes, brushing with the glaze for the last 5–10 minutes. Spoon any remaining glaze over the drumsticks and serve.

lemon and oregano
chicken

serves 4

MARINADE

2 tablespoons extra-virgin olive oil

2 tablespoons dry white wine

6 large cloves garlic, crushed

4–6 teaspoons fresh oregano leaves or 2–3 teaspoons dried oregano

chile flakes or small red chiles (fresh or dried) to taste

1 whole chicken, 4 lb (2 kg), cut into 10 pieces

GARNISH

fresh oregano sprigs

zest from 1 lemon, cut into thin julienne strips

12 oil-cured black olives

12 cracked Sicilian green olives

chile flakes or small red chiles (fresh or dried) to taste

salt to taste

For the marinade, in a large nonaluminum dish, combine the oil, wine, garlic, oregano, and chiles. Stir well. Add the chicken pieces and toss to coat evenly with the marinade. Cover and refrigerate for a few hours or overnight. Remove from the refrigerator 1 hour before cooking.

Turn on broiler (griller) or heat grill (barbecue) to hot.

Place the chicken pieces on cooking rack. Broil, 5–6 inches (13–15 cm) from heat, or grill, until golden around the edges, about 20 minutes. Turn the chicken over and continue to cook until golden brown around the edges and cooked through, about 20 minutes more.

Transfer the chicken to a large serving platter and garnish with oregano sprigs, lemon zest, black and green olives, and chile flakes or chiles. Let the chicken rest for at least 30 minutes to blend the flavors. Sprinkle with salt and serve at room temperature.

serves 4

⅓ cup (½ oz/15 g) packed fresh mint leaves

⅓ cup (½ oz/15 g) packed fresh parsley sprigs, stems removed

⅓ cup (1 oz/30 g) drained, oil-packed, sun-dried tomatoes

¼ cup (2 fl oz/60 ml) olive oil

1 clove garlic, halved

1½ teaspoons finely shredded lemon zest

salt to taste

⅛ teaspoon lemon-pepper seasoning

4 chicken breast halves (1 lb/500 g total), skinless if desired

❖ For the pesto, in a blender container or food processor bowl, combine the mint, parsley, dried tomatoes, olive oil, garlic, lemon zest, salt, and lemon-pepper seasoning. Blend or process until finely chopped. Set aside.

❖ If desired, remove skin from the chicken. Make a pocket in each breast by cutting a 2-inch (5-cm) deep slit just above the breastbone on the meaty side. Fill each pocket with one-fourth of the pesto.

❖ Turn on broiler (griller). Place the chicken, bone-side up, on unheated rack of the broiler pan. Broil (grill), 4–5 inches (10–12 cm) from heat, for 20 minutes. Turn the chicken and broil until cooked through, a further 5–15 minutes.

chicken breasts
with tomato-mint pesto

bacon-wrapped
drumsticks
with plum sauce

serves 4

8 small chicken drumsticks (about 2 lb/1 kg)

salt and pepper to taste

1 small clove garlic, minced (optional)

1 tablespoon vegetable oil

8 slices (rashers) bacon

PLUM SAUCE

½ cup (4 oz/125 g) plum jam

1 tablespoon cider vinegar, or to taste

1 tablespoon mild chile sauce, or to taste

❖ Turn on broiler (griller). Using a sharp knife, cut slashes 1 inch (2.5 cm) apart in meaty part of drumsticks. Rub drumsticks with salt, pepper, and garlic, if using. Brush with oil and place on unheated rack of broiler pan. Broil (grill) 3–4 inches (8–10 cm) from heat for 10 minutes. Turn and brush with oil frequently during cooking. Cool slightly, then wrap a slice of bacon firmly around each drumstick. Secure the ends with toothpicks. Broil until the chicken is cooked through and the bacon is crisp, about 10 minutes more.

❖ For the sauce, gently heat jam, cider vinegar, and chile sauce in a small pan. Mix well and transfer to a small serving bowl. Arrange the hot drumsticks on a serving dish around the dipping sauce.

spicy spanish kabobs

serves 4

¼ cup (2 fl oz/60 ml) olive oil
or vegetable oil

1 tablespoon lemon juice

2 tablespoons chopped flatleaf (Italian)
parsley, plus extra sprigs for garnish

½ teaspoon ground cumin

¼–½ teaspoon cayenne pepper

½ teaspoon dried thyme,
crushed

½ teaspoon paprika

⅛ teaspoon
saffron threads,
crushed, or
ground turmeric

salt and ground
black pepper to taste

12 oz (375 g) chicken thigh meat,
cut into 1-inch (2.5-cm) cubes
or 2- x 1-inch (5- x 2.5-cm) strips

1 large orange, cut into
segments, for garnish

❖ Combine the oil, lemon juice, parsley, cumin, cayenne pepper, thyme, paprika, saffron or turmeric, and salt and pepper. Pour mixture into a heavy-gauge plastic bag, add the chicken, seal bag, and turn to coat chicken evenly. Refrigerate for 4–24 hours, turning bag from time to time. Drain, reserving marinade.

❖ Turn on broiler (griller). Thread chicken pieces on four long metal skewers, leaving about ¼ inch (5 mm) between each one. Place the kabobs on the unheated rack of the broiler pan. Broil (grill) 3–4 inches (8–10 cm) from heat until chicken is cooked through, 10–12 minutes, turning once and brushing with reserved marinade occasionally during cooking. Garnish with parsley sprigs and orange segments.

firecracker
chicken thighs

serves 4–6

*1½–2 lb (750 g–1 kg)
skinless chicken thighs*

*2–3 tablespoons
hot bean paste*

*2 tablespoons
soy sauce*

*2 tablespoons toasted
sesame seeds, crushed*

1 tablespoon sesame oil

1 tablespoon sugar

*¼ cup (¾ oz/20 g) finely
chopped green (spring)
onions*

*4 large cloves garlic,
minced (about 1 tablespoon)*

salt and pepper to taste

*hot cooked rice noodles,
to serve (optional)*

❖ Score the chicken thighs on both sides by making shallow diagonal cuts about 1 inch (2.5 cm) apart.

❖ In a large mixing bowl, stir together the bean paste, soy sauce, sesame seeds, sesame oil, sugar, green onions, garlic, and salt and pepper. Pour mixture into a heavy-gauge plastic bag. Add the chicken pieces. Seal the bag and turn it to coat the chicken evenly. Marinate in the refrigerator for 4–24 hours, turning from time to time. Drain, reserving marinade.

❖ Heat grill (barbecue) to medium heat. Place chicken on the cooking rack and grill for 15 minutes, then turn and cook for a further 10–15 minutes. Baste both sides of meat with reserved marinade and grill until chicken is cooked through, about 5 minutes more, turning once. Discard any remaining marinade. Serve with rice noodles, if desired.

211

chicken salad niçoise

serves 4

DRESSING

2 x 6-oz (185-g) jars marinated artichoke hearts

2 tablespoons balsamic vinegar

1 tablespoon drained capers

1 tablespoon anchovy paste

1 tablespoon Dijon-style mustard

4 cloves garlic, minced

½ teaspoon herbes de Provence

SALAD

12 oz (375 g) skinless, boneless chicken breast halves

spinach or romaine (cos) lettuce leaves

8 tiny new potatoes, cooked and quartered

2 tomatoes, cut into wedges

1 green or red bell pepper (capsicum), cut into strips

2 hard-cooked eggs, sliced

1 fresh fennel bulb, sliced

¼ cup (1 oz/30 g) pitted Niçoise, Kalamata, or other black olives

chicken salad niçoise

❖ For the dressing, drain artichokes, reserving liquid. In a screw-top jar, combine the reserved artichoke liquid, vinegar, capers, anchovy paste, mustard, garlic, and herbes de Provence. Shake well.

❖ For the salad, in a large heavy-gauge plastic bag, combine the chicken and ¼ cup (2 fl oz/60 ml) of the salad dressing. (Cover and chill remaining salad dressing until serving time.) Seal the bag and turn to coat chicken with the dressing. Marinate in the refrigerator for 8–24 hours. Drain marinade from chicken and discard the marinade.

❖ Turn on the broiler (griller). Place chicken on unheated rack of broiler pan. Broil (grill), 5–6 inches (12–15 cm) from heat, for 6–8 minutes per side, or until cooked through. Cool slightly, then slice each chicken breast diagonally. Line a large serving dish with spinach or lettuce leaves. Arrange chicken, artichokes, potatoes, tomatoes, bell pepper strips, eggs, fennel, and olives on the dish and drizzle with remaining dressing. Serve at once.

garlic and ginger poussins

serves 4

4 x 1–1½-lb (500–750-g)
poussins (spatchcocks),
butterflied (see page 200)

3 tablespoons vegetable oil

1 tablespoon peeled and
grated ginger

2 large garlic cloves, minced

1½ teaspoons salt

½ teaspoon black pepper

1 onion, thinly sliced

1 small cucumber, thinly sliced

1 carrot, thinly sliced

2 teaspoons sugar

1½ tablespoons white wine
vinegar

❖ Rub the poussins with a little of the oil. In a small bowl, combine the ginger, garlic, ¾ teaspoon of the salt, and the pepper. Rub the poussins with the mixture. Cover and refrigerate for 1 hour.

❖ Turn on broiler (griller) or heat grill (barbecue) to medium-high. Place poussins on cooking rack skin-side up, if broiling, or skin-side down, if grilling. Broil, 4–5 inches (10–12 cm) from heat, or grill, until golden brown and cooked through, turning and brushing with the remaining oil as needed, 40–50 minutes total.

❖ Place the onion, cucumber, and carrot in a medium dish. In a small bowl, mix the remaining salt, the sugar, and vinegar. Pour the mixture over the vegetables and knead with your fingers until the vegetables soften, 2–3 minutes. Transfer poussins to warmed plates and garnish with the pickled vegetables. Serve immediately.

satay sticks

serves 4–6 as an appetizer

SATAY SAUCE

1 cup (4 oz/125 g) roasted unsalted peanuts

1 tablespoon vegetable oil

1 onion, finely chopped

2 cloves garlic, crushed

2 teaspoons chopped fresh chile

1 tablespoon chopped fresh lemongrass or
2 teaspoons grated lemon or lime zest

2 teaspoons curry powder

1 teaspoon ground cumin

1½ cups (12 fl oz/375 ml) unsweetened
coconut milk

2 tablespoons packed brown sugar

2 teaspoons lime juice

2 lb (1 kg) chicken breast meat,
cut into thin strips

1 tablespoon vegetable oil

cilantro (fresh coriander) sprigs

✧ For the satay sauce, using a food processor, process the peanuts until crushed. Or, place them in a heavy-gauge plastic bag and crush them with a rolling pin.

✧ In a medium frying pan over medium heat, warm the oil. Add the onion, garlic, chile, lemongrass or lemon or lime zest, curry powder, and cumin. Cook, stirring, until the onion is soft, about 3 minutes. Add the peanuts, coconut milk, sugar, and lime juice. Cook, stirring, until hot.

✧ Turn on broiler (griller) or heat grill (barbecue) to medium-high.

✧ Thread the chicken strips onto 12 long metal skewers, leaving about ¼ inch (5 mm) between each piece. Place the skewers on the cooking rack. Brush with the oil and broil, 4 inches (10 cm) from heat, or grill, until golden-brown and cooked through, turning once, 8–10 minutes total.

✧ Serve the chicken skewers on a bed of thinly sliced vegetables, if desired. Pour over the satay sauce.

recipe hint

When making kabobs, it is best to use metal skewers, as wooden ones are inclined to burn. However, if you wish to use wooden skewers, soak them in cold water for at least 1 hour before using.

blackened chicken
with tomato-chile coulis

TOMATO-CHILE COULIS

⅓ cup (2½ fl oz/80 ml) tomato paste

1 tomato, finely chopped

1 tablespoon lime juice

1 tablespoon chile sauce

¼ teaspoon Tabasco sauce

2 teaspoons chopped fresh dill

salt and pepper to taste

6 skinless, boneless chicken breast halves
(1½ lb/750 g total)

1 tablespoon paprika

2 teaspoons black pepper

½ teaspoon cayenne pepper

2 teaspoons garlic powder

2 teaspoons onion powder

1 teaspoon salt

1 teaspoon dried thyme

½ cup (4 oz/125 g) butter, melted

For the coulis, in a small bowl, mix the tomato paste, tomato, lime juice, chile sauce, Tabasco sauce, dill, and salt and pepper. Let stand for at least 1 hour.

Place each chicken breast half between plastic wrap and, using the flat side of a meat mallet, pound until it is of uniform thickness.

In a screw-top jar, combine the paprika, black pepper, cayenne pepper, garlic powder, onion powder, salt, and thyme. Shake well to mix.

Turn on broiler (griller) or heat grill (barbecue) to medium-high.

Dip the chicken into the melted butter and sprinkle both sides with the spice mixture. Place on cooking rack. Broil, 3 inches (7.5 cm) from heat, or grill, until a black crust forms and the chicken is cooked through, 2 minutes on each side. (This cooking process creates a lot of smoke, so have a strong exhaust fan operating if you are cooking indoors.)

Serve the chicken with the tomato coulis.

recipe hint

The spice mix can be made several weeks ahead. Store in an airtight container at room temperature. The sauce can be made a day ahead; cover and refrigerate until needed.

chicken cobb salad

serves 4

ROQUEFORT DRESSING

1/3 cup (3 fl oz/100 ml) buttermilk

3 tablespoons crumbled Roquefort cheese

2 tablespoons mayonnaise

2 tablespoons sour cream

1 tablespoon finely chopped fresh chives

1 teaspoon finely chopped garlic

ground black pepper to taste

SALAD

2 skinless, boneless chicken breast halves (about 8 oz/250 g total)

2 tablespoons extra-virgin olive oil

1 teaspoon chopped fresh tarragon

salt and freshly cracked pepper to taste

8 slices (rashers) bacon

2 hearts of romaine (cos) lettuce, cut into thin ribbons

3/4 cup (4 oz/125 g) diced avocado

3/4 cup (4 oz/125 g) seeded and diced tomato

6 hard-cooked eggs, peeled and diced

2/3 cup (3 oz/90 g) crumbled Roquefort cheese

❖ For the dressing, in a small bowl, combine the buttermilk, Roquefort cheese, mayonnaise, sour cream, chives, garlic, and pepper. Mix until smooth.

❖ Turn on broiler (griller) or heat grill (barbecue) to medium-high.

❖ Brush the chicken breasts with the oil, then sprinkle with the tarragon, salt, and cracked pepper. Place on cooking rack. Broil, 4–5 inches (10–12 cm) from heat, or grill, until cooked through and golden on both sides, about 10 minutes total, turning as needed. Remove from the heat. Allow to cool completely, then dice into ½-inch (10-mm) pieces.

❖ Warm a small frying pan over medium heat. Put the bacon in the hot pan and fry, turning once, until crispy on both sides, 4–6 minutes total. Using tongs, transfer bacon to paper towels to drain. When cool, chop coarsely into ½-inch (10-mm) pieces.

❖ For the salad, place the lettuce on a large platter, mounding it neatly. On top, layer the grilled chicken, avocado, tomato, eggs, Roquefort cheese, and bacon. The lettuce should be hardly visible.

❖ Serve at the table, drizzling the Roquefort dressing over the salad and tossing to coat evenly.

butterflied citrus chicken

serves 4

"Butterflying," or flattening, a whole chicken allows the maximum amount of surface area to be exposed to the broiler (griller) or grill (barbecue), ensuring that the bird cooks evenly.

MARINADE

⅓ cup (3 fl oz/90 ml) olive oil or vegetable oil

⅓ cup (3 fl oz/90 ml) orange juice

¼ cup (2 fl oz/60 ml) lemon juice

1½ teaspoons dried rosemary, crushed

2 cloves garlic, minced

salt and pepper to taste

1 whole chicken, 2½–3 lb (1.25–1.5 kg), butterflied (see page 200)

◈ For the marinade, in a small mixing bowl, stir together the oil, orange juice, lemon juice, rosemary, garlic, and salt and pepper. Pour the marinade into a large, heavy-gauge plastic bag. Add the chicken and seal the bag. Turn the bag to coat the chicken with the marinade. Place in the refrigerator and marinate for 8–24 hours, turning the bag occasionally. Drain the marinade from the chicken, reserving the marinade.

◈ Heat a covered grill (barbecue) to medium-hot.

◈ Place the chicken on the grill rack, skin-side up. Brush with some of the reserved marinade. Cover and cook for 30 minutes. Brush with additional marinade. Cover and cook until cooked through, 30–40 minutes more. Discard any remaining marinade. (Or, if you don't have a covered grill, cook on an open grill over medium-hot coals, but baste with the marinade about every 10 minutes to prevent the meat from drying out.)

◈ Transfer chicken to a platter and serve with roast vegetables or salad, if desired.

japanese kabobs

makes 12
serves 4 as a main course

Serve these kabobs
as appetizers, too—warm
or chilled. Allow 1–2 per
person. When weather
permits, cook them on the
grill (barbecue) instead
of the broiler (griller).

MARINADE

1 teaspoon finely shredded orange zest

1/2 cup (4 fl oz/125 ml) orange juice

1/3 cup (3 fl oz/90 ml) dry sherry

1/4 cup (2 fl oz/60 ml) soy sauce

2 teaspoons sugar

1 clove garlic, minced

1/2 teaspoon peeled and grated fresh ginger

12 oz (375 g) chicken breast meat, cut into
1-inch (2.5-cm) pieces

6–8 green (spring) onions, cut into 1/2-inch
(10-mm) lengths

hot cooked rice

pickled ginger (optional)

✧ For the marinade, in a small mixing bowl, combine the orange zest and juice, the sherry, soy sauce, sugar, garlic, and ginger. Stir. Set aside ¼ cup (2 fl oz/60 ml) of the marinade to serve with the cooked kabobs.

✧ Thread three chicken pieces and two green onion pieces, alternating chicken with onions, onto each of 12 metal skewers, leaving about ¼ inch (5 mm) between each piece. Place the kabobs in a shallow dish and pour the marinade over them. Marinate at room temperature for 30 minutes, turning kabobs once. Remove kabobs from dish. Reserve marinade.

✧ Turn on broiler (griller). Place kabobs on rack of broiler pan. Broil 4 inches (10 cm) from the heat until the chicken is cooked through, 8–10 minutes, turning and brushing with reserved marinade once.

✧ In a small saucepan over medium heat, bring the ¼ cup (2 fl oz/60 ml) reserved marinade to a boil. Serve the hot marinade with the kabobs, rice, and pickled ginger, if desired.

tapatia-style
enchiladas

makes 24
serves 8

Ancho chiles are large, broad, dried chiles with a slightly sweet flavor. They are not very hot. They can be very difficult to get, so you can use any large, mild chile for this recipe. Generally, the larger the chile, the milder it is. (This is a very general rule—it is always a good idea to check the heat of chiles before buying them.)

CHILE SAUCE

8–10 ancho chiles, ribs and stems removed

warm water as needed

3 tablespoons vegetable oil

1 small onion, chopped

2 small cloves garlic, minced

salt and pepper to taste

*3 boneless, skinless chicken breast halves
(12 oz/375 g total)*

ENCHILADAS

½ cup (4 fl oz/125 ml) vegetable oil

24 small (3-inch/7.5-cm) tortillas

1 cup (8 fl oz/250 ml) sour cream, or to taste

8 oz (250 g) añejo cheese or dry feta, crumbled

For the chile sauce, in a small bowl, combine the chiles and warm water to cover. Soak for about 10 minutes. Drain, place in a food processor or blender, and process or blend, adding enough of the soaking liquid to make a thin purée.

In a medium saucepan over medium-high heat, warm 2 tablespoons of the oil. Add the onion and garlic and sauté until translucent, about 3 minutes. Strain the chile purée into the pan and add the salt and pepper. Reduce heat to low and simmer for about 10 minutes. The sauce should be just thick enough to coat a wooden spoon. If it thickens too much, add a little water to thin. Keep warm.

Turn on broiler (griller). Brush the chicken breasts with the remaining oil. Place, skin-side down, on rack of broiler pan. Broil (grill), 4–5 inches (10–13 cm) from the heat, until cooked through and golden on both sides, about 10 minutes total, turning as needed. Remove from the heat. Allow to cool completely, then shred the meat.

For the enchiladas, in a medium frying pan over medium-high heat, warm the oil. Immerse the tortillas one at a time, for a few seconds on each side, until they fold easily. Then dip both sides in the chile sauce and fill with a little chicken. Fold in half and place on a serving dish. Repeat with the rest of the enchiladas and filling.

Spoon the rest of the sauce over the prepared enchiladas and top with the sour cream and cheese. Serve immediately.

lettuce-wrapped
thai thighs

makes 24
serves 12 as an appetizer

6 cilantro (fresh coriander) stems with roots

3 tablespoons fish sauce

1 tablespoon oyster sauce

2 cloves garlic, peeled

8 boneless chicken thighs (about 2 lb/
1 kg total)

SAUCE

2 cups (1 lb/500 g) sugar

1 cup (8 fl oz/250 ml) water

1 small red bell pepper (capsicum), cut in
half, seeds reserved

4 cloves garlic, peeled

3 tablespoons fish sauce

⅓ cup (3 fl oz/90 ml) lemon juice

1 teaspoon salt

1 teaspoon Tabasco sauce

TO FINISH

8 oz (250 g) soba noodles, cooked and
drained

1 bunch cilantro (fresh coriander) sprigs

1 bunch mint sprigs

1 head lettuce, leaves separated

1 bunch chives

❖ Using a food processor, process the cilantro stems and roots, fish sauce, oyster sauce, and garlic until a smooth paste forms. Place the chicken thighs in a large bowl and turn to coat with the paste. Cover and refrigerate for several hours or overnight.

❖ Heat grill (barbecue) to medium-hot.

❖ Place the chicken, skin-side up, on the grill rack. Grill for 5 minutes, then turn and grill until skin is crisp and chicken is cooked through, about 5 minutes more. Cool, then cut each thigh into four long strips.

❖ For the sauce, in a small saucepan over high heat, bring the sugar and water to a boil, stirring until the sugar dissolves. Boil rapidly for 10 minutes. Remove from the heat and cool completely. Transfer to a small bowl. Using a food processor, process the bell pepper, garlic, and ½ cup (4 oz/125 g) of the sugar syrup until smooth. (Discard any leftover syrup.) Add the fish sauce, lemon juice, salt, and Tabasco sauce and process until blended.

❖ Place one strip of chicken, some noodles, cilantro, and mint in a lettuce leaf. Tie it together with one chive. Repeat to make about 24 "parcels" and arrange them on a platter. Serve with the sauce for dipping.

grilled kabobs

makes **12**

serves 4 as a main course
or 6–12 as an appetizer

The yogurt in this classic
marinade tenderizes the
chicken, yielding succulent
results. If you like, grill
(barbecue) vegetables on
separate skewers. Serve the
kabobs with pita bread and
make a simple sauce of
yogurt and finely chopped
cucumber to spoon over the
chicken and vegetables.

1 large yellow onion, chopped

4 cloves garlic, minced

1/4 cup (2 fl oz/60 ml) fresh lemon juice

1 tablespoon paprika

1/2 teaspoon ground cayenne pepper

1/2 teaspoon ground black pepper

1 tablespoon chopped fresh thyme

1 cup (8 oz/250 g) plain yogurt

1 1/2 lb (750 g) chicken breast or thigh meat,
cut into 1-inch (2.5-cm) cubes

olive oil, for brushing

salt and pepper to taste

❖ Using a food processor, process the onion, garlic, lemon juice, paprika, cayenne pepper, ½ teaspoon black pepper, and thyme until combined. Add the yogurt and process to mix.

❖ Place the chicken in a nonaluminum container. Add the yogurt mixture and stir to coat the chicken with the marinade. Cover and refrigerate for 8 hours or overnight.

❖ Turn on broiler (griller) or heat grill (barbecue) to medium-hot.

❖ Remove the chicken pieces from the marinade. Reserve marinade. Thread the chicken onto 12 metal skewers, leaving about ¼ inch (5 mm) between each piece. Brush the chicken with oil and sprinkle with salt and pepper.

❖ Place the skewers on the cooking rack. Broil, 4 inches (10 cm) from heat, or grill until cooked through, 4–5 minutes each side for breast meat and 5–6 minutes each side for thigh meat, turning and basting once with the reserved marinade. Discard excess marinade.

❖ Transfer the skewers to warmed individual plates or a serving platter. Serve hot.

mexican marinated chicken

serves 4

Mexican cooks often marinate chicken in citrus juices before grilling (barbecuing). Don't marinate the meat longer than overnight, however, or it will become too soft.

1 cup (8 fl oz/250 ml) fresh orange juice

2 tablespoons fresh lime juice

1 dried chipotle chile, stemmed and seeded

1 cup (8 fl oz/250 ml) salsa (tomato and chile pickle)

¼ cup (2 fl oz/60 ml) olive oil

1 teaspoon salt

4 skinless, boneless chicken breast halves (1 lb/500 g total)

fresh orange slices (optional)

cilantro (fresh coriander) sprigs (optional)

◈ In a small saucepan over high heat, combine the orange juice, lime juice, and chile. Bring to a boil. Reduce heat to low and simmer, uncovered, until chile is plump, about 5 minutes. Remove the pan from the heat and allow to cool.

◈ In the bowl of a food processor, combine the cooled mixture, the salsa, oil, and salt. Process to a purée.

◈ Place the chicken breasts in a shallow nonaluminum dish. Pour the purée evenly over the chicken. Cover and marinate in the refrigerator for 2–4 hours.

◈ Turn on broiler (griller) or heat grill (barbecue) to hot.

◈ Remove the chicken breasts from the marinade. Discard marinade. Place chicken breasts on the cooking rack, skin-side down if broiling and skin-side up if grilling. Broil, 4 inches (10 cm) from heat, or grill, for 2–3 minutes each side. Continue to cook, turning every 2–3 minutes to avoid burning, until cooked through, 12–20 minutes total.

◈ Transfer the chicken to a warmed platter. Garnish with orange slices and cilantro sprigs, if desired. Serve immediately.

five-spice chicken

serves 4

2 small chickens, about 2 lb (1 kg) each

MARINADE

1 inch (2.5 cm) piece fresh ginger, peeled
and grated

4 cloves garlic, chopped

2 shallots, chopped

1 1/2 tablespoons brown sugar

salt and freshly ground black pepper
to taste

1/2 teaspoon five-spice powder

2 tablespoons Vietnamese or Thai fish sauce

2 tablespoons soy sauce

1 tablespoon dry sherry

FISH SAUCE AND LIME DIPPING SAUCE

1 clove garlic, finely minced

1 small red chile, seeded and finely minced

1/4 cup (2 oz/60 g) sugar

1/4 cup (2 fl oz/60 ml) fresh lime juice,
including pulp

1/3 cup (2 1/2 fl oz/80 ml) Vietnamese or
Thai fish sauce

1/2 cup (4 fl oz/125 ml) water

❖ Using poultry or kitchen shears, cut each chicken in half through the breastbone and backbone. Using your palms, press down on the breasts to flatten the halves slightly.

❖ For the marinade, using a mortar and pestle or mini food processor, grind or process the ginger, garlic, shallots, sugar, and salt to a smooth paste. Transfer to a large shallow bowl. Add the pepper, five-spice powder, fish sauce, soy sauce, and sherry. Mix well. Add the chicken halves and turn to coat thoroughly with the marinade. Cover and marinate in the refrigerator for a few hours or as long as overnight.

❖ For the dipping sauce, using a food processor, process the garlic, chile, and sugar to form a paste. Add the lime juice and pulp, fish sauce, and water and stir to dissolve the sugar. Strain the sauce into a bowl or jar. Use immediately, or cover and refrigerate for up to 5 days.

❖ Heat grill (barbecue) to very hot. Transfer the chicken halves to grill rack, bone-side down, and grill for about 20 minutes. Turn the chicken over and continue to grill until cooked through and golden brown, about 20 minutes more.

❖ Serve hot with the dipping sauce.

grilled
chicken with aïoli

serves 4

2 baby chickens (Cornish game hens),
about 1¾ lb (875 g) each

½ cup (4 fl oz/125 ml) olive oil

¼ cup (2 fl oz/60 ml) lemon juice

2 cloves garlic, crushed

4 green (spring) onions, chopped

1 tablespoon chopped fresh thyme

AÏOLI

2 egg yolks

¼ teaspoon salt

2 cloves garlic, crushed

⅔ cup (5 fl oz/150 ml) vegetable oil

⅓ cup (3 fl oz/90 ml) olive oil

1 tablespoon lemon juice

4 thin Oriental (lady finger) eggplants
(aubergines), thinly sliced lengthwise

2 green zucchini (courgettes), thinly sliced
lengthwise

2 yellow squash zucchini (courgettes), thinly
sliced lengthwise

2 red bell peppers (capsicums), cut into
thick strips

4 red-skinned potatoes, thinly sliced

coarse salt to taste

ground black pepper to taste

❖ Using poultry or kitchen shears or a sharp knife, cut along either side of the backbone of each chicken. Remove and discard backbones. Place the chickens breast-side up on a work surface and flatten with your hand. In a small bowl, combine the oil, lemon juice, garlic, green onions, and thyme. Brush the chickens with some of the mixture.

❖ The chickens may be grilled (barbecued) or baked. If grilling, heat a covered grill (barbecue) to low. Place chicken halves on the unheated grilling rack. Grill until cooked through, about 30 minutes, turning once. Or, bake the chickens in a preheated 375°F (190°C/Gas Mark 4) oven for about 30 minutes, or until almost cooked through. Finish the chickens under a hot broiler (griller) to brown them.

❖ For the aïoli, using a food processor, process the egg yolks, salt, and garlic until smooth. With the motor running, gradually add the oils in a thin stream until the mixture is thick. Transfer to a small bowl. Add the lemon juice and stir well.

❖ Brush the eggplants, zucchini, bell peppers, and potatoes with some of the oil mixture. Grill until well browned and tender, about 10 minutes. Drizzle with the remaining oil mixture and sprinkle with salt and pepper. Serve the chicken with the vegetables and aïoli.

braising,
stewing,
and
casseroling

braising, stewing, and casseroling basics

Braising, stewing, and casseroling are all methods of slow, moist cooking. Braising begins with sautéing the food to brown the outside and seal in juices. Then a little liquid is added and the food is covered and slowly cooked. This develops the flavors and tenderizes the meat. There is just enough liquid to stop the food from drying out and to serve as a base for a sauce. Braising can be done on the stovetop or in the oven.

When stewing, food is only just covered by liquid (much more than is used when braising) and is covered and simmered on the stovetop for up to several hours. The juices from the meat and the liquid combine to form a sauce or a gravy. Like braising, this method develops the flavors and tenderizes the meat. The meat may or may not be browned before being cooked, and it is usually in smaller pieces than for braising.

For casseroling, the food may or may not be browned first, before being slowly oven-cooked in a casserole dish. A casserole dish is a deep, usually round, ovenproof dish with a tight-fitting lid. It can be made of any heatproof material. A casserole also has handles and the food can be served straight from the oven to the table. A Dutch oven can also be used for braising, stewing, and casseroling. This is a large, heavy pot, usually made from cast iron, with a tight-fitting lid. It can be used in the same way that you would use a flameproof casserole.

braising, stewing, and casseroling basics

Even though these cooking methods are slower than other methods, they don't demand much from you after preparation is completed and cooking begins. You only need to check the temperature every now and then and occasionally check and, if needed, replenish the cooking liquid. These methods of cooking are ideal for entertaining because, while the food is cooking, you are free to attend to other details of the dinner, or just relax. Also, food that is cooked in these ways actually improves with sitting because it allows the flavors to further develop.

Another advantage of using these methods of cooking is that they can be almost complete meals in themselves. The vegetables are often cooked in the same dish and all that is needed is an accompaniment, such as noodles, rice, or potatoes, to soak up the sauce or gravy—and some dishes may only require some thick crusty bread to accompany them. They are also excellent choices for low-fat diets because skinless chicken will not dry out and you need very little added fat to bring out the flavors.

Also, you can use stewing chickens quite successfully with these cooking methods. Stewing chickens are usually older and tougher than other chickens, but they are also more flavorful. These methods of cooking gently break down the fibers and tenderize the tougher meat.

There are a couple of key points to ensure successful braising, stewing, and casseroling. The first and probably the most important is to have a tight-fitting lid. This prevents any liquid from escaping as steam and is essential to producing a moist, tender meal. Also, when browning the meat prior to slow cooking, don't crowd the pieces in the pan or they won't develop a good, even color. The equipment you will need for all three cooking methods may vary, or they may be all the same. If you have a flameproof casserole dish or a Dutch oven, then you can use this for all three cooking methods. If you are using a frying pan to brown the meat before oven braising, be sure that your frying pan has heatproof handles and lid.

port, pear, and fig
casserole

3 tablespoons butter

*4 skinless chicken legs
(about 2 lb/1 kg total)*

4 green (spring) onions, chopped

½ cup (4 fl oz/125 ml) dry red wine

½ cup (4 fl oz/125 ml) port

1 cup (8 fl oz/250 ml) chicken stock

2 small pears, quartered

*1 tablespoon cornstarch (cornflour)
blended with 1 tablespoon cold water*

*⅔ cup (3 oz/90 g) chunky
cranberry sauce*

4 fresh figs, quartered

1 tablespoon chopped fresh chives

◈ In a large frying pan over medium heat, melt the butter. Add the chicken legs and cook until well browned, about 5 minutes total. Remove the chicken from the pan and drain any excess fat from the pan. Add the green onions, wine, port, and stock and bring to a boil. Return the chicken to the pan. Reduce heat to low, cover, and simmer for 10 minutes.

◈ Add the pears to the pan. Cover and simmer until tender, a further 10 minutes. Add the cornstarch mixture and cook, stirring, until the mixture boils and thickens, 3–5 minutes more. Add the cranberry sauce, figs, and chives and stir gently until hot. Serve immediately.

hearty
coq au vin

CROUTONS

4 slices French bread

1 tablespoon olive oil

1 clove garlic, peeled and halved

COQ AU VIN

1 tablespoon margarine or butter

1 tablespoon vegetable oil

2 lb (1 kg) meaty chicken pieces (breasts, thighs, and drumsticks), skinned if desired

salt and pepper to taste

1½ cups (6 oz/185 g) fresh mushrooms, cut into quarters

12 pearl (pickling) onions, peeled

2 slices (rashers) bacon, chopped

2 cloves garlic, minced

2 tablespoons all-purpose (plain) flour

1 cup (8 fl oz/250 ml) chicken stock

1 cup (8 fl oz/250 ml) dry red wine

2 tablespoons tomato paste

1 tomato, peeled, seeded, and chopped

3 tablespoons chopped fresh parsley

1 tablespoon chopped fresh tarragon or 1 teaspoon dried tarragon, crushed

1 bay leaf

◈ Preheat oven to 300°F (150°C/Gas Mark 2).

◈ For the croutons, lightly brush both sides of the bread slices with the olive oil. Rub with the cut side of the garlic halves. Cut the bread slices into ¾–1-inch (2–2.5-cm) pieces. Place the bread cubes in a shallow baking dish. Bake until crisp, about 15 minutes, turning once. Remove from the oven and allow to cool.

◈ Increase oven temperature to 350°F (180°C/Gas Mark 4).

◈ For the coq au vin, in a large, ovenproof, heavy-based frying pan or a Dutch oven over medium heat, warm the margarine or butter and oil. Add the chicken and brown on all sides, about 5 minutes total. Remove the chicken from the pan. Sprinkle with salt and pepper.

◈ Add the mushrooms, onions, bacon, and garlic to the pan. Cook until the mushrooms are tender and the bacon and onions are soft, about 5 minutes. Drain fat from the pan, leaving about 2 tablespoons in the bottom of the pan. Add the flour and cook, stirring, for 1 minute. Add the stock, wine, tomato paste, chopped tomato, 1 tablespoon of the parsley, the tarragon, and bay leaf. Return the chicken to the pan and bring to a boil. Cover, place in oven, and bake for 45 minutes.

◈ Before serving, remove the bay leaf. If necessary, skim off excess fat. Transfer to serving plates. Serve each portion topped with some of the croutons and the remaining parsley.

alsatian chicken and dumplings

1 tablespoon vegetable oil

2 lb (1 kg) meaty chicken pieces (breasts, thighs, and drumsticks), skinned if desired

1/2 cup (3 oz/90 g) chopped onion

1 lb (500 g) shredded cabbage

14 oz (440 g) can tomatoes, diced

1 small green bell pepper (capsicum), chopped

1–2 tablespoons packed brown sugar

1 teaspoon caraway seeds

salt and pepper to taste

1 cup (8 fl oz/250 ml) dry white wine, apple juice, or apple cider

1 cup (8 fl oz/250 ml) chicken stock

DUMPLINGS

1/3 cup (1 1/2 oz/45 g) all-purpose (plain) flour

1/3 cup (1 1/2 oz/45 g) cornmeal (polenta)

1 teaspoon baking powder

salt to taste

1/2 cup (4 fl oz/125 ml) milk

2 tablespoons vegetable oil

2 slices (rashers) bacon, crisp-cooked and crumbled

1 tablespoon chopped fresh parsley, plus extra for garnish

✧ In a large, heavy-based frying pan or a Dutch oven over medium heat, warm the oil. Add the chicken and brown on all sides, about 5 minutes total. Remove the chicken from the pan. Add the onion to the pan and cook until crisp-tender, 2–3 minutes. Add the cabbage, undrained tomatoes, bell pepper, sugar, caraway seeds, and salt and pepper. Stir in the wine, apple juice, or apple cider. Bring to a boil. Return chicken to the pan. Reduce heat to low, cover, and simmer for 30 minutes. Stir in the stock. Return mixture to a boil.

✧ While the chicken is simmering, make the dumplings. In a medium bowl, stir together the flour, cornmeal, baking powder, and salt. In a small bowl, combine the milk and vegetable oil. Add to the dry ingredients and, using a fork, mix well. Stir in the bacon and the 1 tablespoon parsley. Using a tablespoon, scoop up 1 heaping spoonful of the mixture and, using another spoon to push the mixture off, drop 1 dumpling atop the boiling stew. Make 6 dumplings in total. Reduce heat to low. Cover and simmer, without lifting the lid, until the dumplings are cooked, 10–12 minutes. (To test, insert a toothpick into the center of a dumpling; if it comes out clean, the dumpling is cooked.) Garnish with the extra chopped parsley and serve at once.

spicy yogurt chicken

serves 4

This recipe uses
low-fat yogurt and only
2 tablespoons of margarine
or butter, making it a very
healthful, light dish.
But even though it is good
for you, it still has a rich,
intense flavor.

MARINADE

1 cup (8 fl oz/250 ml) plain low-fat yogurt

2 tablespoons chopped cilantro (fresh coriander) or
fresh parsley, plus extra for garnish

1 tablespoon curry powder

2 cloves garlic, minced

1 teaspoon ground ginger

1 teaspoon paprika

2–3 teaspoons lime juice or lemon juice

salt to taste

4 skinless chicken legs (about 2 lb/1 kg total)

2 tablespoons margarine or butter

For the marinade, in a small mixing bowl, stir together the yogurt, the 2 tablespoons cilantro or parsley, the curry powder, garlic, ginger, paprika, lime or lemon juice, and salt.

Place the chicken legs in a large, heavy-gauge plastic bag set into a shallow dish. Pour the marinade into the bag. Seal the bag and turn it to coat the chicken completely with marinade. Marinate in the refrigerator for 2–24 hours, turning the bag occasionally.

In a large frying pan over medium heat, melt the margarine or butter. Add the chicken legs and the marinade and bring to a boil. Reduce heat to low, cover, and simmer until the chicken is cooked through, 45–50 minutes.

Transfer the chicken to a serving platter. Bring the marinade to a boil and gently boil until slightly thickened, about 5 minutes. Pour over the chicken and garnish with the extra cilantro or parsley. Serve hot.

recipe hint

To allow the marinade to penetrate the chicken, score the meat before it is marinated. Do this by using a sharp knife to make shallow parallel marks in the meatiest part of each leg. Then marinate as usual.

serves 6

2 tablespoons vegetable oil

2–2½ lb (1–1.25) kg chicken breasts, thighs, and/or drumsticks, skinned if desired

1½ cups (12 fl oz/375 ml) water

⅓ cup (3 fl oz/80 ml) cider vinegar

2 tablespoons soy sauce

3 large cloves garlic, minced

½ teaspoon whole peppercorns

½ teaspoon ground black pepper

1 bay leaf

1 medium green bell pepper (capsicum), thinly sliced

2 tablespoons cornstarch (cornflour), mixed with 2 tablespoons water

1 cup (8 fl oz/250 ml) tinned unsweetened coconut milk

hot cooked rice

¼ cup (¾ oz/20 g) sliced green (spring) onions

❖ In a large, heavy-based frying pan over medium-high heat, warm the oil. When hot, add chicken and cook, turning to brown evenly. Drain off fat.

❖ Add water, vinegar, soy sauce, garlic, peppercorns, pepper, and bay leaf to the pan. Bring to a boil, reduce heat, then cover and simmer until chicken is cooked through, about 30 minutes. Add the bell pepper during the last 5 minutes.

❖ Transfer chicken to a serving dish and keep warm. Remove bell pepper and set aside.

❖ Stir the cornstarch mixture into the pan juices. Cook, stirring, until thick and bubbly. Continue cooking and stirring for 2 minutes more. Add to the pan the coconut milk and bell pepper. Stir in and heat through, but do not boil.

❖ Divide the rice among serving plates, top with the chicken, and spoon the sauce over. Sprinkle with spring onions.

chicken filipino-style

hearty
chicken casserole

serves 6

2 tablespoons vegetable oil

4 lb (2 kg) chicken pieces

2 onions, sliced lengthwise

2 cloves garlic, crushed

8 oz (250 g) thinly sliced
speck or prosciutto

3 carrots, thickly sliced

2 stalks celery, thickly sliced

14 oz (440 g)
canned crushed tomatoes

1/3 cup (3 fl oz/90 ml)
tomato paste

1 cup (8 fl oz/250 ml)
chicken stock

1 x 1-lb (500-g)
can cannellini beans,
rinsed and drained

1/3 cup (1/3 oz/10 g)
chopped fresh basil

2 tablespoons chopped
fresh oregano

❖ In a large frying pan over high heat, warm the oil. Add some of the chicken pieces and fry, turning to brown evenly, about 5 minutes total. Do not cook through. Transfer to a plate. Repeat in batches with the remaining chicken.

❖ Reduce heat to medium and add the onions, garlic, speck or prosciutto, carrots, and celery. Cook, stirring, until the onions are soft, about 5 minutes. Add the tomatoes, tomato paste, and stock. Bring to a boil, return the chicken to the pan, then reduce heat and simmer, uncovered, until the chicken is cooked through, about 15 minutes. Add the beans and herbs and simmer for 2–3 minutes. Divide among warmed bowls and serve immediately.

chicken rouladen

serves 4

4 skinless, boneless chicken breast halves (about 1 lb/500 g)

4 teaspoons honey mustard or Dijon-style mustard

4 slices thinly sliced fully cooked ham (about 1½ oz/45 g)

1 x 7¼-oz (220-g) jar roasted red bell peppers (capsicums), drained

1 tablespoon vegetable oil

½ cup (4 fl oz/125 ml) chicken stock

½ cup (4 fl oz/125 ml) dry white wine

2 tablespoons tomato paste

1 tablespoon chopped fresh basil or ½ teaspoon dried basil, crushed

2 tablespoons cornstarch (cornflour), mixed with 1 tablespoon water

❖ Place each chicken breast between two pieces of plastic wrap. Using the flat side of a meat mallet and working from the center to the edges, lightly pound each piece to a ¼-inch (5-mm) thickness. Remove plastic wrap.

❖ Spread each piece of chicken with 1 teaspoon of mustard. Place a slice of ham on each, then a bell pepper half.

Fold in the ends of the chicken pieces then roll up, jelly-roll (Swiss-roll) style. Secure with toothpicks.

❖ In a large, heavy-based frying pan over medium heat, warm the oil. Add the chicken rolls and brown on all sides. Add the stock and wine and bring to a boil. Reduce heat, cover, and simmer until chicken is cooked through, about 30 minutes. Remove chicken from the pan and keep warm.

❖ Stir the tomato paste and basil into the pan juices. Stir the cornstarch mixture into the pan. Cook, stirring, until thick and bubbly, then continue cooking for a further 1–2 minutes.

❖ With a sharp knife, slice each roll into ½-inch (1-cm) slices and divide between warmed serving plates. Spoon the sauce over. Serve immediately.

chicken couscous

serves 4–5

1 tablespoon olive or vegetable oil

½ cup (2 oz/60 g) chopped onion

1 clove garlic, minced

12 oz (375 g) chicken thigh meat, cut into
1-inch (2.5-cm) cubes

3 carrots, cut into 1-inch (2.5-cm) pieces

1¼ cups (10 fl oz/310 ml) chicken stock

1 cup (2 oz/60 g) sliced celery

salt to taste

¼ teaspoon ground turmeric

¼ teaspoon ground cumin

⅛–¼ teaspoon cayenne pepper

1 medium zucchini (courgette), cut into
½- x ½- x 1-inch (1-cm x 1-cm x 2.5-cm) strips

2 tomatoes, peeled, seeded, and chopped

1 x 15-oz (470-g) can chickpeas
(garbanzo beans), drained

1 cup (6 oz/180 g) couscous

✤ In a large, heavy-based frying pan or Dutch oven over medium heat, warm the oil. Add the onion and garlic and cook, stirring, until tender but not brown, about 5 minutes. Add the chicken, carrots, stock, celery, salt, turmeric, cumin, and cayenne pepper. Bring to a boil, reduce heat, cover, and simmer for 20 minutes.

✤ Add the zucchini, tomatoes, and chickpeas. Cover and cook until chicken is cooked through and vegetables are tender, about 10 minutes more.

✤ Meanwhile, prepare couscous according to package directions. Spoon couscous into serving bowls. Spoon chicken mixture over couscous and serve.

chicken curry
with three accompaniments

serves 4

¼ cup (2 oz/60 g) ghee (clarified butter)

2 lb (1 kg) skinless, boneless chicken breasts, sliced

2 onions, chopped

3 cloves garlic, minced

2 teaspoons peeled and grated fresh ginger

1 tablespoon curry powder

1 teaspoon turmeric

2 teaspoons ground cumin

1 teaspoon garam masala

½ teaspoon chopped fresh chile

1 x 13-oz (410-g) can tomatoes

1 cup (8 fl oz/250 ml) chicken stock

2 cups (16 fl oz/500 ml) unsweetened coconut cream

1 green bell pepper (capsicum), chopped

8 oz (250 g) cauliflower, chopped

3 Oriental (lady finger) eggplants (aubergines), chopped

1 tablespoon chopped cilantro (fresh coriander)

THREE ACCOMPANIMENTS

½ cup (4 fl oz/125 ml) plain yogurt

1 small green cucumber, finely chopped

1 tablespoon chopped fresh mint

2 small tomatoes, finely chopped

1 tablespoon lime juice

1 tablespoon chopped cilantro (fresh coriander)

⅓ cup (3 oz/100 g) mango chutney

chicken curry with three accompaniments

To serve the curry in individual bowls, you will need four ovenproof 2-cup (500-ml) serving dishes. The curry and accompaniments can be made a day ahead. If making ahead, gently reheat the curry in a saucepan or microwave oven until hot. Refrigerate the accompaniments until shortly before serving time.

❖ In a large frying pan, heat 3 tablespoons of the ghee over high heat. Add a few chicken slices and cook, stirring, over high heat until golden brown. Transfer the cooked chicken to a plate. Repeat in batches with the remaining chicken slices.

❖ Preheat oven to 450°F (230°C/Gas Mark 6).

❖ Add to the pan the remaining ghee, the onions, garlic, ginger, curry powder, turmeric, cumin, garam masala, and chile. Cook over medium heat, stirring, until the onion is soft and the spices fragrant, about 5 minutes. Add the tomatoes, stock, and coconut cream. Bring to a boil. Add the vegetables, reduce heat, and simmer, uncovered, until vegetables are tender and sauce is thick, about 20 minutes.

❖ Return the chicken to the pan and simmer until the chicken is cooked through, about 10 minutes. Stir in the cilantro.

chicken curry with three accompaniments

❖ For the three accompaniments, combine the yogurt, cucumber, and mint in a small bowl and mix well. Combine the tomatoes, lime juice, and cilantro in another small bowl and mix well. Place the mango chutney in another small bowl.

❖ Serve the chicken curry immediately with the three accompaniments.

recipe variations

There are many options for accompaniments to this curry. Try the following:
Slice a banana and sprinkle it with flaked coconut.
Combine the following for a tangy, hot pickle: sliced pickled lime, green (spring) onions, and fresh chile.
Fry some peanuts or almonds in oil, drain on paper towels, and sprinkle with salt.

chicken cassoulet

cassoulet

serves 6

Cassoulet is a French country dish containing beans and meat in a variety of combinations, depending on regional preference. A *cassoulet* is always covered and cooked slowly. To make preparation easier, use 15 oz (470 g) canned white beans instead of the dried; you don't need to cook the beans and you can use water in place of the reserved bean liquid.

1½ cups (7 oz/220 g) dried great Northern beans, or any white beans

8 cups (2 qt/2 l) water

4 green (spring) onions, sliced

1 bunch fresh parsley, chopped

⅓ cup (2½ fl oz/80 ml) dry red or white wine

2 slices (rashers) bacon, crisp-cooked and crumbled

1 tablespoon tomato paste

3 cloves garlic, minced

½ teaspoon dried thyme, crushed

1 bay leaf

6 chicken drumsticks or thighs (about 1½ lb/750 g total)

1 tablespoon olive oil or vegetable oil

8 oz (250 g) fully cooked Polish sausage (kielbasa) or any smoked pork sausage, sliced into 1-inch (2.5-cm) pieces

◈ Preheat oven to 350°F (180°C/Gas Mark 4).

◈ In a large saucepan or Dutch oven, combine the beans and 4 cups (1 qt/1 liter) of the water. Bring to a boil. Reduce heat and simmer for 2 minutes. Let stand, covered, for 1 hour. (Or, soak beans in 4 cups/1 qt/1 liter water overnight.) Drain the beans, discarding the water. In the same pan, combine the beans and the remaining water. Bring to a boil. Reduce heat and simmer until beans are tender, 12 hours. Drain, reserving ⅔ cup (5 fl oz/160 ml) of the liquid.

◈ In a large mixing bowl, stir together the drained beans, reserved bean liquid, green onions, parsley, wine, bacon, tomato paste, garlic, thyme, and bay leaf.

◈ In a large, heavy-based frying pan over medium-high heat, warm the oil. Add the chicken and fry, turning to brown evenly, for about 5 minutes total. In a Dutch oven or ovenproof casserole, layer one-third of the beans, all of the chicken, and all of the sausage. Top with the remaining bean mixture. Cover and place in the oven. Bake until the chicken and the beans are cooked through, 40–45 minutes.

◈ Remove from the oven and let stand for 5 minutes. Serve in warmed bowls with thick crusty white bread.

balsamic chicken

serves 4

Oyster mushrooms, asparagus, and pine nuts give crunch and snap to this delicious, simple braise. Oyster mushrooms are an Asian variety with pale, creamy flesh and a flowerlike cap.

2 tablespoons olive oil or vegetable oil

4 skinless, boneless chicken breast halves (1 lb/500 g total)

white pepper to taste

3 shallots or green (spring) onions

1 cup (8 fl oz/250 ml) chicken stock

12 oz (375 g) fresh asparagus spears or 10 oz (315 g) frozen asparagus spears, trimmed and cut into 2-inch (5-cm) lengths

2 cups (4 oz/125 g) fresh oyster mushrooms or other mushrooms, or any large mushrooms, halved

3 tablespoons balsamic vinegar

2 tablespoons margarine or butter, softened

2 tablespoons toasted pine nuts

hot cooked rice

❖ In a large, heavy-based frying pan over medium-high heat, warm the oil. Add the chicken and cook for 2 minutes. Turn chicken over and sprinkle with pepper. Add shallots or green onions and cook for a further 2 minutes. Drain off any fat. Add the chicken stock. Bring to a boil, then reduce heat, cover, and simmer for 5 minutes.

❖ Add the asparagus to the pan. Cover and cook until asparagus is just tender and chicken is cooked through, 5–7 minutes. Add the mushrooms. Cover and cook for 1 minute more.

❖ Using a slotted spoon, transfer the chicken, asparagus, and mushrooms to a serving platter. Add the vinegar to the liquid in the pan. Increase heat to high. Bring to a boil and boil until the liquid is reduced to ⅓ cup (3 fl oz/90 ml), about 5 minutes. Remove the pan from heat. Using a wire whisk, blend the margarine or butter into the liquid in the pan. Spoon the liquid over the chicken. Sprinkle with the pine nuts. Serve with rice.

goulash

serves 4

Serving a dish made with potatoes over noodles is common in Eastern European cuisine. The flavors and textures mesh beautifully.

Spaetzle, a tiny German dumpling, is available in most well-stocked supermarkets in the pasta section.

1–2 tablespoons vegetable oil

12 oz (375 g) chicken thigh meat, cut into 1-inch (2.5-cm) pieces

1 small onion, chopped

1 clove garlic, minced

2 potatoes, peeled and diced

7 oz (220 g) canned chopped tomatoes, juice reserved

¼ cup (2 fl oz/60 ml) water

1½ teaspoons paprika

¼ teaspoon caraway seeds

¼ teaspoon dried marjoram, crushed

pinch of dried thyme, crushed

salt and pepper to taste

2 tablespoons all-purpose (plain) flour

2 tablespoons water

hot cooked noodles or spaetzle

sour cream to taste (optional)

In a large, heavy-based frying pan over medium-high heat, warm 1 tablespoon of the oil. Add the chicken, onion, and garlic and cook until chicken is cooked through, about 5 minutes. Drain off fat. Add the potatoes, tomatoes, ¼ cup (2 fl oz/20 ml) water, paprika, caraway seeds, marjoram, thyme, and salt and pepper. Bring to a boil, then reduce heat, cover, and simmer until the potatoes are tender, 10–12 minutes.

In a small bowl, stir together the flour and 2 tablespoons water. Stir into the pan. Cook, stirring, until thick and bubbly, 3–4 minutes. Cook, stirring, for 1 minute more. Serve over hot cooked noodles or *spaetzle*, with sour cream, if desired.

recipe hint

Goulash is a traditional Hungarian dish and it is worthwhile using good pungent, Hungarian paprika. Most supermarkets stock mild paprika, but if you can track down Hungarian paprika, you will have a much more interesting and authentic dish.

chicken
with kaffir lime leaf

serves 4

2 oz (60 g) tamarind pulp, coarsely chopped

1 cup (8 fl oz/250 ml) boiling water

SPICE PASTE

1 x ½-inch (12-mm) piece fresh galangal, chopped; or 1 piece dried galangal (¼ inch/6 mm), soaked in water for 30 minutes then chopped

1 lemongrass stalk, tender heart section only, coarsely chopped

4 shallots or 1 yellow onion, quartered

5 small red chiles, seeded

3 cloves garlic, peeled

1 teaspoon ground turmeric

3 tablespoons water, or as needed

¼ cup (2 fl oz/60 ml) vegetable oil

1 whole chicken, about 2 lb (1 kg), cut into serving pieces

1 cup (8 fl oz/250 ml) coconut milk

6 kaffir lime or other citrus leaves or the zest of 1 lime

1 teaspoon salt, or to taste

✧ In a small bowl, soak the tamarind pulp in the boiling water for 15 minutes. Using the back of a fork, mash to help dissolve the pulp. Pour through a fine-mesh sieve into another small bowl, pressing against the pulp to extract as much liquid as possible. Discard the pulp and reserve the tamarind liquid.

✧ For the spice paste, using a blender or food processor, blend or process the galangal, lemongrass, shallots or onion, chiles, garlic, turmeric, and 3 tablespoons water to a smooth paste, adding more water if needed.

✧ In a large saucepan over medium heat, warm the oil. Add the spice paste and fry, stirring, until fragrant, thick, and creamy, about 3 minutes. Continue cooking, stirring, until the oil separates from the paste, about 5 minutes. Add the chicken pieces and fry, turning often, until fully coated with the spice paste, about 3 minutes. Stir the reserved tamarind liquid into the pan and bring to a boil. Reduce heat to medium and simmer, uncovered, turning occasionally, for 15 minutes. Add the coconut milk, lime or citrus leaves or zest, and salt. Simmer until the chicken is cooked through, about 10 minutes more. Serve hot.

oloroso sherry chicken

serves 4

1 whole chicken,
about 2 lb (1 kg)

2 cloves garlic, peeled

⅓ cup (3 fl oz/90 ml) olive oil,
plus 1 teaspoon extra

1 lb (500 g) onions,
finely chopped

6½ oz (200 g) carrots, sliced

1⅔ cups (13 fl oz/410 ml)
Oloroso sherry

salt and freshly ground pepper
to taste

10 oz (315 g) button
mushrooms (champignons),
chopped

✧ Rub the chicken inside and out with the garlic.
In a large heatproof casserole or large saucepan over
medium heat, warm most of the oil. Add the chicken
and fry until it starts to brown, turning occasionally,
about 5 minutes total. Add the onions and carrots.
Reduce heat to low and cook, stirring occasionally, for
15 minutes. Add the sherry. Increase heat to high and
cook for a further 3 minutes to burn off the alcohol.
Add salt and pepper and reduce heat to low. Cover
and cook for 45 minutes, turning 2 or 3 times.

✧ In a small frying pan over high heat, warm the
remaining oil. Add the mushrooms and sauté until soft,
about 5 minutes.

✧ Quarter the chicken. Cool pan juices slightly, then
purée in a blender. Line a platter with mushrooms,
arrange chicken on top, and pour sauce over. Serve hot.

almond chicken

⅓ cup (3 fl oz/90 ml) olive oil

1 thick slice bread (1 oz/30 g)

10 almonds

2 cloves garlic, peeled

1 whole chicken, about 3 lb (1.5 kg),
chopped into 10 pieces

1 onion, finely chopped

2¾ cups (20 fl oz/600 ml) water

1 teaspoon lemon juice

salt to taste

1 pinch ground cinnamon

1 pinch ground cloves

1 pinch saffron

1 pinch cumin seeds

2 hard-cooked egg yolks

✦ In a large heatproof casserole or large saucepan over medium heat, warm the oil. Add the bread, almonds, and garlic and fry until browned, about 3 minutes. Remove from the pan. Add the chicken and fry until golden-brown, about 5 minutes total. Remove from the pan. Add the onion and fry until soft, 5 minutes. Return the chicken to the pan and cover with water. Add the lemon juice, salt, cinnamon, and cloves. Reduce heat to low. Cover and cook until chicken is cooked through, 45–60 minutes.

✦ Using a mortar and pestle, crush the saffron, cumin seeds, fried bread, garlic, and almonds. Add the hardcooked egg yolks, dilute with a little of the cooking water, and mix to a paste. Add the paste to the chicken and stir to make a thick sauce, about 3 minutes. Serve hot.

boiling, steaming, *and* poaching

boiling, steaming, and poaching basics

B oiling is a method of cooking food in a boiling liquid—one in which bubbles break the surface. Most foods are boiled for only short periods of time. Boiling is a common way to cook starchy foods such as potatoes and pasta, or to reduce liquid. It is also often a step in poaching chicken—the liquid must be brought to a boil before reducing the heat to a simmer to poach the chicken. Boiling is also used to make stock. By rapidly boiling, much of the flavor and nutrients are drawn out of the chicken into the liquid, to be used as stock.

As boiling tends to make meat tough, chicken is usually simmered or poached. Poaching is a delicate method of cooking that bathes the food in gently bubbling liquid just below a boil. The result is moist, succulent meat with a light clean flavor that is ideal for salads, sandwiches, and soups. It is low in fat because no oil is used. It is also very flavorsome, because the poaching liquid draws flavor from the meat and bones, and can also infuse the meat with its own flavor.

The key to perfectly poached chicken is to keep the heat at a constant temperature throughout cooking. For the most delicious result, select a pot made from a material that will heat evenly and maintain temperature. It should also be large enough to allow the hot liquid to move freely around the chicken pieces.

Steaming, on the other hand, is the method that retains most of the chicken's flavor, texture, and nutrients. In this method, food is placed in a steamer—basically an open rack over boiling or simmering liquid—and the steamer is covered to prevent steam from escaping. The food is cooked by the heat of the steam. There are many types of steamers, from Asian bamboo steamers, to electric steamers, and stovetop steamers. It really doesn't matter what type of steamer you use, as long as it has a good tight-fitting lid to stop the steam from escaping and it is large enough to fit all the food in—ideally, in only one layer.

After chicken has been steamed or poached, it is a good idea to allow it to sit at room temperature for about 15 minutes. This allows the chicken to cool so that it can be handled, and it also recirculates the juices so they don't pour out when the meat is cut.

To remove the skin and bones from cooked chicken, place it on a cutting board. Pull off the skin and discard. The meat should be tender enough that it will come away from the bone with just a little tug. If not, cut it away with a knife—however, if it is too difficult to pull away, then it is probably undercooked and needs more cooking time. Once the skin is removed and the meat is taken off the bone, the cooked chicken can be cut up to suit any recipe. Make sure you always use a sharp knife. To shred cooked chicken meat, steady the meat with a fork and pull the fibers apart with a second fork. Remember to always go with the grain of the meat—this will give you fine shreds of chicken meat ready for use in soups or salads.

saffron
bouillabaisse

serves 4

MARINADE

3 tablespoons olive oil

2 leeks, trimmed and sliced

2 cloves garlic, crushed

6 large sticks celery, thickly sliced

14 oz (440 g) canned tomatoes, undrained and crushed

1/3 cup (3 fl oz/90 ml) Pernod or Ricard

1/4 teaspoon powdered saffron or saffron threads

1 tablespoon chopped fresh thyme

2 tablespoons chopped fresh dill

4 skinless chicken legs (2 lb/1 kg total)

3 cups (24 fl oz/750 ml) chicken stock

Tabasco sauce and salt and pepper to taste

❖ For the marinade, in a large non-metallic dish, combine the oil, leeks, garlic, celery, tomatoes, Pernod or Ricard, saffron, thyme, and dill. Mix well. Add the chicken legs and stir to coat. Cover and refrigerate overnight.

❖ Pour the chicken and the marinade into a large saucepan over medium heat. Bring to a boil, then reduce heat, cover, and simmer for 15 minutes. Add the chicken stock. Cover and simmer until the chicken is cooked through, a further 15 minutes. Add salt, pepper, and Tabasco before serving.

❖ This recipe is best prepared a day ahead and reheated gently just before serving.

thai-style soup

serves 4 as a main course
or 8 as an appetizer

Lemongrass is available from
Asian food stores. If you
cannot find it, substitute
2 teaspoons of grated lime
zest. Fish sauce is also
available from Asian food
stores, but light soy sauce
may be substituted.

2 tablespoons vegetable oil

2 onions, chopped

3 cloves garlic, crushed

2 teaspoons ground cumin

1 teaspoon turmeric

1 teaspoon chopped chile

1 tablespoon chopped fresh lemongrass

¼ cup (2 fl oz/60 ml) lime juice

4 cups (1 qt/1 liter) chicken stock

2 cups (16 fl oz/500 ml) unsweetened coconut cream

2 tablespoons Thai or Vietnamese fish sauce

1 lb (500 g) chicken breast meat, thinly sliced

2 tablespoons chopped cilantro (fresh coriander)

lime leaves, for garnish

In a medium frying pan over medium heat, warm the oil. Add the onion and garlic and cook, stirring, until the onion is soft, about 5 minutes. Add the cumin, turmeric, chile, and lemongrass and cook, stirring, until the lemongrass is tender, about 5 minutes more. Add the lime juice, stock, coconut cream, and fish sauce and bring to a boil. Stir in the chicken. Simmer, uncovered, until the chicken is cooked through, about 5 minutes. Stir in the cilantro and cook until hot.

Ladle soup into individual bowls and serve at once.

recipe variations

If you prefer not to use coconut cream, replace it with 2 cups (8 fl oz/250 ml) vegetable stock. Add more or less chile, to taste, and also add a 1-inch (2.5-cm) piece of peeled minced ginger or galangal at the same time as the garlic. This makes a delicious, tangy soup.

hearty chicken soup with dumplings

½ cup (4 oz/125 g) pearl barley

8 oz (250 g) frozen lima (broad) beans

2 tablespoons vegetable oil

2 lb (1 kg) chicken breast meat, sliced

3 leeks, trimmed and sliced

2 cloves garlic, crushed

3 stalks celery, chopped

3 carrots, chopped

2 zucchini (courgettes), chopped

8 cups (2 qt/2 l) chicken stock

½ cup tomato paste

DUMPLINGS

¾ cup (3 oz/90 g) all-purpose (plain) flour

3 tablespoons cornmeal (polenta)

1½ teaspoons baking powder

salt to taste

½ cup (2 oz/60 g) grated Parmesan cheese

⅓ cup (3 oz/90 g) cold butter, grated

½ cup (4 fl oz/125 ml) water, or as needed

1 small bunch chopped fresh flatleaf (Italian) parsley

1 tablespoon chopped fresh thyme

salt and pepper to taste

Rinse the barley under cold water until the water runs clear. Drain. Pour boiling water over the beans, then drain. When cool enough to handle, remove skins.

In a large saucepan over medium-high heat, warm the oil. Add the chicken, in batches, and cook until well browned all over, about 5 minutes. Add the leek, garlic, celery, carrot, and zucchini. Cook, stirring, until the leeks are soft, about 5 minutes. Add the stock and tomato paste and bring to a boil. Add the barley and simmer, covered, for 20 minutes. Return the chicken to the pan with the beans.

For the dumplings, in a bowl, combine the flour, cornmeal, baking powder, and salt. Stir in the cheese and butter. Add enough water to form a soft dough. Using a tablespoon, drop level spoons of dumpling mixture into the simmering soup. Cover and simmer until the dumplings are cooked through and the barley is tender, about 15 minutes more.

Stir in the parsley, thyme, and salt and pepper. Transfer to soup bowls and serve immediately.

recipe hint

The soup can be prepared a day ahead; however, the barley will thicken the soup overnight, so if a thinner consistency is desired, add a little extra water or stock when reheating. Dumplings are best made just before serving. To test if they are cooked, insert a toothpick into the center of a dumpling. If it comes out clean, the dumpling is cooked.

spicy chicken and corn soup

serves 4 as a main course
or 8 as an appetizer

1 tablespoon vegetable oil

1 lb (500 g) chicken breast meat, sliced

5 oz (150 g) chorizo sausage, chopped

2 onions, chopped

2 cloves garlic, crushed

1 tablespoon ground cumin

1/4 teaspoon chile powder

3 cups (24 fl oz/750 ml) chicken stock

3 cups (24 fl oz/750 ml) tomato juice

2 1/2 tablespoons tomato paste

2 teaspoons sugar

1 red and 1 green bell pepper (capsicum), chopped

2 zucchini (courgettes), chopped

12 oz (340 g) canned red kidney beans, rinsed and drained

12 oz (340 g) canned corn kernels, drained

2 1/2 tablespoons chopped cilantro (fresh coriander)

salt and pepper to taste

❖ In a large frying pan over medium-high heat, warm the oil. Add the chicken and chorizo and cook, stirring, until lightly browned, about 5 minutes. Remove from pan and set aside.

❖ Add the onion and garlic to the pan. Cook, stirring, until onion is soft, about 5 minutes. Add the cumin and chile and cook, stirring, until fragrant, about 1 minute. Add the stock, tomato juice, tomato paste, and sugar. Bring to a boil.

❖ Add the bell peppers and zucchini and simmer, uncovered, until just tender, about 5 minutes. Stir in the chicken, beans, corn, and cilantro. Simmer, uncovered, until hot.

❖ Add salt and pepper. Serve immediately.

creamy chicken salad

DRESSING

3 tablespoons olive oil

1 onion, finely chopped

2 teaspoons curry powder

1 tablespoon apricot jelly or jam

1 tablespoon mango chutney

¼ cup (1 oz/30 g) unsalted macadamia nuts

2 tablespoons raspberry vinegar

½ cup (4 fl oz/125 ml) mayonnaise

¼ cup (2 fl oz/60 ml) light (single) cream

4 skinless, boneless chicken breast halves (about 1 lb/500 g), poached until tender, cooled

1 bunch (3 oz/90 g) arugula (rocket), stemmed

2 large mangoes, peeled, pitted, and sliced

2 large avocados, peeled, pitted, and sliced

1 bunch fresh chives, cut into 2-inch (5-cm) lengths

◈ For the dressing, in a small saucepan over medium heat, warm 1 tablespoon of the oil. Add the onion and cook until translucent, about 3 minutes. Add the curry powder and cook, stirring, for 1 minute. Remove from the heat and stir in the apricot jelly or jam and mango chutney. Mix well. Allow to cool. In a blender or food processor, blend or process the macadamia nuts briefly until chopped. Add the remaining oil and the vinegar and process until well combined. Add the nut mixture to the cooled onion mixture. Stir in the mayonnaise and cream. Mix well.

◈ Slice each chicken breast half lengthwise into 5–6 strips. Arrange the arugula, chicken, mango, and avocado on individual serving dishes. Spoon some dressing onto each serving.

◈ Garnish with the chives and serve immediately.

parmesan gougère

serves 6

GOUGÈRE

1 cup (8 fl oz/250 ml) water

½ cup (4 oz/125 g) butter or margarine

salt to taste

1 cup (4 oz/125 g) all-purpose (plain) flour

4 eggs

⅔ cup (3 oz/90 g) finely grated Parmesan cheese

FILLING

2 tablespoons margarine or butter

3 carrots, thinly sliced

1 cup (2 oz/60 g) quartered fresh mushrooms

2 zucchini (courgettes), sliced

1 onion chopped

¾ cup (6 fl oz/190 ml) chicken stock

2 tablespoons all-purpose (plain) flour

1 teaspoon dried Italian seasoning, crushed

salt and pepper to taste

2 cups (5 oz/155 g) chopped cooked chicken meat

½ cup (2 oz/60 g) shredded provolone or mozzarella cheese

1 tomato, peeled, seeded, and chopped

◈ Preheat oven to 400°C (200°F/Gas Mark 5).

◈ For the *gougère*, in a medium saucepan over medium heat, combine the water, butter or margarine, and salt. Bring to a boil. Add the flour, all at once, stirring vigorously. Cook, stirring, until the mixture forms a ball that does not separate, about 5 minutes. Remove the pan from heat. Cool for 10 minutes. Add the eggs, one at a time, beating with a wooden spoon until smooth after each addition. Stir in ½ cup (2 oz/60 g) of the Parmesan cheese. Spread the mixture over the bottom and up the sides of a well-greased, deep 10-inch (25-cm) pie dish. Sprinkle with the remaining Parmesan cheese. Bake until golden brown, 30–40 minutes.

◈ For the filling, in a large frying pan over medium heat, melt the margarine or butter. Add the carrots, mushrooms, zucchini, and onion. Cook, stirring, until the vegetables are just tender, about 5 minutes.

◈ In a medium mixing bowl, stir together the stock, flour, Italian seasoning, and salt and pepper. Add to the mixture in the frying pan and cook, stirring, until thick and bubbly. Cook, stirring, for 1 minute further. Stir in the cooked chicken, provolone or mozzarella cheese, and tomato. Heat through. Fill the hot *gougère* shell with the hot filling. Serve immediately.

taipei chicken

serves 4

2 cups (5 oz/155 g) shredded poached or
steamed chicken, still warm

4 oz (125 g) crisp chow mein noodles

3 tablespoons thinly sliced green (spring) onions

¼ cup (2 fl oz/60 ml) soy sauce

2 tablespoons toasted sesame oil

2 tablespoons rice vinegar

2 tablespoons water

2 teaspoons sugar

2 teaspoons peeled and grated fresh ginger

1 tablespoon seeded and finely chopped red or
green jalapeño or other chile

2 cups (2 oz/60 g) mixed fresh salad greens

❖ In a large mixing bowl, combine the chicken, noodles, and green onions.

❖ In a small saucepan over medium heat, stir together the soy sauce, sesame oil, vinegar, water, sugar, ginger, and chile. Bring to a boil, stirring to dissolve the sugar. Remove from heat and pour over the chicken mixture. Toss to coat. Serve atop the fresh mixed salad greens.

curried chicken
salad

serves 4 as a main course
or 6 as an appetizer

2 tablespoons chutney

1/2 cup (3 oz/90 g) mayonnaise
or salad dressing

1/2 teaspoon curry powder

1/2 cup (3 oz/90 g) lightly
salted whole almonds

2 cups (5 oz/155 g)
chopped cooked chicken

2 red or green unpeeled pears,
cored and coarsely chopped

spinach leaves, for lining

◈ Chop any large pieces of fruit in the chutney.
In a small mixing bowl, stir together the chutney,
mayonnaise or salad dressing, and curry powder.

◈ Coarsely chop 2 oz (60 g) of the almonds. In a large
mixing bowl, combine the chicken, pears, and chopped
almonds. Add the mayonnaise mixture and mix well.
Cover and chill for 2–24 hours.

◈ Line individual plates with spinach leaves. Place
the salad on the leaves and garnish with the remaining
almonds. Serve immediately.

chicken and cheese tamales

makes 12–14 tamales
serves 6–7

FILLING

4 chicken breast halves
(about 1 lb/500 g total)

2 cups (16 fl oz/500 ml) chicken stock,
or as needed

4 chiles, roasted, peeled, seeded, and cut
lengthwise into strips 2 inches (5 cm) wide

1/2 cup (4 fl oz/125 ml) green salsa

salt and ground black pepper to taste

TAMALE DOUGH

4 fresh chiles, roasted, peeled, and seeded

1/2 cup (4 fl oz/125 ml) green salsa

1 teaspoon baking soda (bicarbonate
of soda)

2 1/2 teaspoons salt

1 1/2 lb (750 g) prepared masa dough
(see note, page 288), chilled

1/2 cup (4 oz/125 g) lard or vegetable
shortening, chilled

1 package (8 oz/250 g) dried corn husks,
soaked in hot water for at least 2 hours

8 oz (250 g) semi-soft, melting cheese,
such as panela, Manchego, or Monterey
jack, cut into thin strips 1/4 inch (6 mm)
thick and 2 inches (5 cm) long

green salsa and light (single) cream
or sour cream, to serve

❖ For the filling, place the chicken breast halves in a large saucepan and add stock to cover. Bring to a boil, then reduce heat to low and simmer, uncovered, until cooked through, about 15 minutes. Using a slotted spoon, transfer the chicken to a plate to cool. Reserve 1 cup (8 fl oz/250 ml) of the stock. Remove the meat from the chicken bones, discard the skin and, using your fingers, shred the meat into 2-inch (5-cm) strips. Place the chicken in a bowl and add the chiles, salsa, and salt and pepper. Toss to mix.

❖ For the dough, using a blender, blend 2 of the chiles, the salsa, reserved stock, baking soda, and salt until smooth. Place the *masa* dough in a bowl and, using an electric mixer on medium speed, beat until light in texture, about 5 minutes. Slowly add the stock mixture, beating until combined. Increase the speed to high and add the lard or shortening, 1 tablespoon at a time. Continue beating until light and fluffy, about 15 minutes.

❖ To make the tamales, drain the corn husks and pat dry. Spread 1 large, or slightly overlap 2 small, softened husks on a work surface, with the narrow end(s) pointing away from you. Leaving about 3 inches (7.5 cm) uncovered at the top and 1½ inches (4 cm) uncovered at the bottom, spread about 2½ tablespoons of the *masa* mixture over the center area of the husk(s). Place a spoonful of the chicken mixture on the *masa* and place 2 or 3 cheese strips on top. Fold one long side of the husk covered with *masa* over the chicken and cheese to enclose the filling completely in *masa* and then fold the opposite long side back over the center. Fold the top down and the bottom up, overlapping the ends. Tie a long shred of a corn husk around the

chicken and cheese tamales

Some version of these steamed packets is served in every region in Mexico. Pack each tamale generously and don't worry if they ooze slightly during cooking. *Masa* dough consists of corn kernels soaked with lime. If it is unavailable, substitute 3 cups (10 oz/315 g) *masa harina* (tortilla flour) mixed with 2 cups (16 fl oz/500 ml) warm water to make a soft dough. Then proceed as directed in the recipe.

center to secure the ends. Wrap in aluminum foil. Repeat with the remaining ingredients.

❖ Line a large steamer rack with the remaining corn husks and arrange the wrapped tamales on it. Place the rack over (not touching) simmering water in a pan. Cover and steam until the husks pull away from the *masa* without sticking, about 1¼ hours. (During cooking, check the level of water in the pan frequently, adding more boiling water as needed to maintain the original level.)

❖ To serve, remove the aluminum foil and place two tamales on each plate. Serve the salsa and the cream or sour cream in bowls on the side. Allow guests to unwrap the parcels at the table.

chef's salad

serves 4

VINAIGRETTE

2 tablespoons fresh lemon juice

2 teaspoons Dijon-style mustard

1 teaspoon finely minced shallot

salt and freshly ground pepper to taste

¼ cup (2 fl oz/60 ml) vegetable oil

2 tablespoons extra-virgin olive oil

SALAD

2 heads lettuce, pale inner leaves only, torn into bite-size pieces

5 oz (155 g) honey-baked ham, cut into julienne strips

5 oz (155 g) smoked chicken or roast turkey, cut into julienne strips

8 oz (250 g) Monterey Jack or Swiss cheese, cut into julienne strips

8 red or yellow cherry tomatoes, quartered

3 hard-cooked eggs, quartered

✧ For the vinaigrette, in a small bowl, whisk together the lemon juice, mustard, shallot, and salt and pepper. Slowly pour in the vegetable oil and olive oil, whisking continuously. Whisk until emulsified, 10–20 seconds.

✧ For the salad, place the lettuce in a large salad bowl or four individual salad bowls. Arrange the ham, chicken or turkey, and cheese on top, keeping each ingredient separate and radiating the strips outward from the center of the bowl. Place the tomato and egg in between the meats and cheese.

✧ Serve the salad with the vinaigrette on the side. Dress and toss at the table.

chinese sesame salad

serves 6

2 large whole chicken breasts
(about 1½ lb/750 g total)

2 teaspoons salt

8 oz (250 g) fresh Chinese egg noodles

1½ teaspoons peanut oil

3 tablespoons white or black sesame seeds

¼ cup (1 oz/30 g) finely julienned
red bell pepper (capsicum)

1 cup (4 oz/125 g) finely julienned carrot

½ cup (½ oz/15 g) cilantro (fresh coriander)
leaves

1 small cucumber, cut into 2-inch (5-cm)
julienne strips

PEANUT-SESAME DRESSING

2 teaspoons peanut butter

2 teaspoons Asian sesame paste

2 tablespoons sugar

⅓ cup (3 fl oz/90 ml) dark soy sauce

⅓ cup (3 fl oz/90 ml) Chinese red vinegar
or balsamic vinegar

2 tablespoons peanut or corn oil

1 tablespoon Asian sesame oil

½ teaspoon chile oil, or to taste

2 teaspoons minced garlic

1 teaspoon peeled and minced fresh ginger

¼ cup (¾ oz/20 g) chopped green
(spring) onion

¼ cup (1 oz/30 g) chopped dry-roasted
peanuts

❖ Fill a large saucepan three-fourths full with water and bring to a boil over medium heat. Add the chicken breasts and return to a boil, skimming off any scum that forms on the surface. Reduce heat to low and simmer, uncovered, until tender, 20–25 minutes. Drain and let cool.

❖ Remove the skin from the chicken breasts, bone them, and hand shred the meat into strips about ½ inch (12 mm) thick and 2 inches (5 cm) long.

❖ Refill the saucepan three-fourths full with water and bring to a boil over high heat. Add the salt. Gently pull the strands of noodles apart, then drop them into the boiling water, stirring to separate the strands. When the water comes to a second boil, boil for 1 minute further. Pour the noodles into a colander and rinse thoroughly with cold running water. Drain thoroughly and transfer to a large bowl. Toss with the peanut oil to keep the noodles from sticking together.

❖ If using white sesame seeds, toast them in a small, dry frying pan over medium heat until golden and fragrant, about 3 minutes. If using black sesame seeds, leave them untoasted.

❖ In a large bowl, toss together the chicken, bell pepper, carrot, cilantro, and sesame seeds. Arrange the cooked noodles in a wide shallow bowl. Scatter the cucumber over the noodles and top with the chicken mixture. Cover and refrigerate until ready to serve.

❖ For the dressing, in a small bowl, stir together the peanut butter, sesame paste, sugar, soy sauce, and vinegar. In a small saucepan over medium heat, warm the peanut or corn oil, sesame oil, and chile oil. Add the garlic, ginger, and green onion and sauté until fragrant, about 15 seconds. Stir in the peanut butter-sesame paste mixture and cook until it begins to form a light syrup, about 1 minute. Remove from the heat and let cool to lukewarm.

❖ Pour the warm dressing over the salad and sprinkle with the peanuts. Serve immediately.

serves 4–6

SAUCE

1½ tablespoons sesame paste

1 tablespoon chile oil

¾ teaspoon sugar

1 tablespoon light soy sauce

1 teaspoon aromatic or apple vinegar

2 tablespoons chicken stock

½ chicken, about 1½ lb (750 g)

2 teaspoons salt

1 tablespoon Chinese rice wine or dry sherry

1 teaspoon sesame oil

1 tablespoon sesame seeds

8 oz (250 g) shredded cucumber

1 red bell pepper (capsicum), shredded

❖ For the sauce, combine the sesame paste, chile oil, sugar, soy sauce, vinegar, and stock.

❖ Rub chicken with the salt, wine or sherry, and sesame oil. Bring a large pan of water to a boil, place the chicken on a steaming rack, and steam over medium heat for 18–20 minutes. Remove, drain, and allow to cool. When cool, bone and shred the meat. Set aside.

❖ In a wok or frying pan over low heat, lightly brown the sesame seeds. Remove from the pan and set aside.

❖ Place the cucumber on a serving dish. Arrange the chicken on top and sprinkle with the bell pepper and sesame seeds. Pour the sauce on top and serve.

bon-bon
chicken

chicken noodle
vegetable soup

serves 4

6 cups (1½ qt/1.5 l)
chicken stock

1 yellow onion, finely
chopped

2 carrots, peeled, halved
lengthwise, and thinly sliced

2 celery stalks, thinly sliced

2 zucchinis (courgettes),
thinly sliced

2 tablespoons finely
chopped fresh flatleaf
(Italian) parsley

2 oz (60 g) dried very thin
egg noodles

½ cup (3 oz/90 g) shredded
or cubed, skinless cooked
chicken meat

salt and ground black
pepper to taste

❖ In a large saucepan over medium-low heat, bring the stock to a simmer, then add the onion, carrots, and celery. Continue to simmer until vegetables are slightly soft, about 10 minutes. Add zucchini and half the parsley and cook until the zucchini is just tender, a further 10 minutes.

❖ Add the noodles and simmer until just tender, 3–4 minutes, or according to package directions.

❖ Three minutes before the noodles are done, add the chicken and cook, stirring, until heated through. Add salt and pepper to taste.

❖ Ladle into warmed soup bowls and sprinkle with the remaining parsley. Serve immediately.

island chicken
sandwiches

serves 4–6

1 chicken,
3–3½ lb (1.5–1.75 kg),
cut into 4–6 pieces

6 cups (1½ qt/1.5 l) water

1 teaspoon finely shredded lime zest

¼ cup (2 fl oz/60 ml) fresh lime juice

salt to taste

¼ teaspoon lemon pepper

¼ cup (1 oz/30 g) flaked dried coconut

½ cup (1½ oz/40 g)
finely chopped green (spring) onions

2 jalapeños or other chiles,
finely chopped

4–6 pita bread rounds or flour tortillas

spinach leaves and/or peeled and sliced
papaya (pawpaw) or mango

❖ In a Dutch oven or heavy-based saucepan, place the chicken and water and bring to a boil. Reduce heat and simmer, covered, until chicken is cooked through, about 40 minutes. Remove chicken from the pan and set aside to cool. When cool, skin, bone, and shred the meat.

❖ In a large mixing bowl, combine and mix chicken, lime zest, lime juice, salt, and lemon pepper. Stir in coconut, green onion, and chiles.

❖ Line pita pockets or tortillas with spinach and/or papaya or mango and add the chicken mixture. Roll up the tortillas, if using. Transfer to a plate and serve soon after preparing.

poached chicken
with star anise and ginger

serves 6

2 cups (16 fl oz/500 ml)
water

¾ cup (6 fl oz/190 ml)
soy sauce

½ cup (3½ oz/105 g)
packed brown sugar

3 tablespoons ginger
liqueur or dry white wine

1 tablespoon peeled and
thinly sliced fresh ginger

2 whole star anise

1 chicken, 3–3½ lb
(1.5–1.75 kg), cut into 6 pieces

hot cooked rice, to serve

❖ In a Dutch oven or heavy-based saucepan, combine the water, soy sauce, brown sugar, ginger liqueur or wine, ginger, and star anise. Place the chicken, skin-side down, in the Dutch oven or saucepan. Bring to a boil. Reduce heat and simmer, covered, for 25 minutes. Turn chicken over and simmer, covered, until cooked through, a further 25–30 minutes. Baste frequently during the last 10 minutes. Remove chicken from the pan and keep warm.

❖ Skim the fat from the pan juices. Strain juices through several layers of 100 percent cotton cheesecloth (muslin). Discard ginger; reserve star anise for garnish, if desired. Reserve 1½ cups (12 fl oz/375 ml) of the liquid. Return reserved liquid to the pan and boil, uncovered, until reduced to ½ cup (4 fl oz/125 ml), 3–4 minutes.

❖ Serve atop hot rice and spoon some of the reserved liquid over the chicken. Garnish with reserved star anise, if desired.

chicken potstickers

makes about 24
serves 4–6

WRAPPERS

2 cups (10 oz/315 g) all-purpose (plain) flour, plus extra as needed

¼ teaspoon salt

¾ cup (6 fl oz/180 ml) boiling water

FILLING

2 cups (6 oz/185 g) finely chopped Chinese (napa) cabbage

¼ cup (1½ oz/45 g) blanched spinach, chopped

1 lb (500 g) ground (minced) dark chicken meat

½ teaspoon peeled and grated fresh ginger

2 tablespoons finely chopped garlic

chives or green (spring) onion

1 teaspoon salt

½ teaspoon sugar

¼ teaspoon ground white pepper

1 tablespoon light soy sauce

1 tablespoon Chinese rice wine or dry sherry

1 teaspoon Asian sesame oil

1½ teaspoons cornstarch (cornflour)

DIPPING SAUCE

6 tablespoons (3 fl oz/90 ml) distilled white vinegar

3 tablespoons light soy sauce

chile oil

vegetable oil for frying

chicken potstickers

❖ For the wrappers, in a food processor, combine the flour and salt and pulse once to mix. With the motor running, slowly pour in the boiling water. Continue to process until a rough ball forms and the dough pulls away from the sides of the work bowl, 15–20 seconds. Transfer to a floured work surface. Knead until smooth and no longer sticky, about 2 minutes. Cover with a kitchen towel and let rest for 30 minutes.

❖ Meanwhile, make the filling. Place the cabbage and spinach in a kitchen towel, wring out excess liquid, and place in a bowl. Add the remaining ingredients and mix until combined. Cover and refrigerate.

❖ Uncover the dough and knead briefly. Cut in half. Roll out one half about ⅛ inch (3 mm) thick. Using a round cookie cutter 3½ inches (9 cm) in diameter, cut out rounds. Repeat with the remaining dough and all scraps, keeping rounds lightly covered with the kitchen towel.

❖ To make the sauce, stir together the vinegar and soy sauce. Add chile oil to taste. Set aside.

❖ Remove the filling from the refrigerator and place 1 tablespoon in the middle of a dough round. Fold the round in half and pinch the edges together at one end of the arc. Starting from that point, make six pleats or tucks along the curved edge to enclose the filling. As each potsticker is made, place it, seam-side up, on a baking sheet, pressing down gently until it sits flat. Continue forming and placing the potstickers.

chicken potstickers

❖ Heat a frying pan over medium-high heat. When hot, add about 2 teaspoons vegetable oil. Arrange 8–10 potstickers, seam-side up and just touching. Fry until the bottoms are browned, about 1 minute. Add water to come halfway up the sides of the potstickers and bring to a boil. Immediately cover, reduce the heat to low, and cook for 8 minutes, adding more water if necessary. Uncover, increase the heat to high, and cook until the liquid is absorbed and the bottoms are crispy, about 30 seconds more. Transfer to a serving dish and keep warm. Fry the remaining potstickers in the same way.

❖ Divide the dipping sauce among individual saucers. Serve the potstickers hot, with the sauce.

thai coconut and chicken soup

serves 6–8

8 kaffir lime leaves or the zest of 1 lime

2 x 12-fl oz (375-ml) cans coconut milk

2 cups (16 fl oz/500 ml) chicken stock

6 fresh or 4 dried galangal slices, each
about 1 inch (2.5 cm) in diameter

4 lemongrass stalks, cut into
2-inch (5-cm) lengths and crushed

4 small green chiles, halved

1 tablespoon Thai roasted chile paste
(nam prik pao) (see page 305)

1 whole skinless, boneless chicken breast
(about 12 oz/375 g), cut into ½-inch
(12-mm) cubes

½ cup (2½ oz/75 g) drained, canned
whole straw mushrooms

½ cup (2½ oz/75 g) drained, canned
sliced bamboo shoots

¼ cup (2 fl oz/60 ml) Thai fish sauce

juice of 2 limes (about 3 fl oz/90 ml)

¼ cup (¼ oz/7 g) cilantro (fresh coriander)
leaves

In a large saucepan over medium-high heat, mix 4 of the lime leaves or half of the zest, the coconut milk, stock, galangal, lemongrass, and chiles. Bring to a boil. Reduce heat to low and simmer, uncovered, for 20 minutes. Strain through a fine-mesh sieve into a clean large saucepan. Discard the contents of the sieve.

Increase heat to medium-high. Bring the strained liquid to a boil. Reduce heat to medium and, when liquid is at a gentle boil, add the remaining kaffir lime leaves or zest, roasted chile paste, chicken, mushrooms, bamboo shoots, and fish sauce. Boil gently until the chicken is cooked through, about 3 minutes. Stir in the lime juice and cilantro. Ladle into warmed bowls and serve hot.

recipe hint

You can make your own roasted chile paste, or *nam prik pao*. Wrap 10 dried red chiles in aluminum foil and roast in a dry frying pan over medium-high heat for about 3 minutes each side. Set aside. In the same pan, combine 1 tablespoon vegetable oil, 1 tablespoon chopped garlic, 3 tablespoons chopped onion, and 1 tablespoon shrimp paste and fry until browned. Add the chiles, 1 tablespoon brown sugar, and 1 teaspoon tamarind concentrate. In a blender or food processor, blend or process to a paste. Use immediately, or store in an airtight container in the refrigerator for up to 2 weeks.

chiang mai
noodle soup

1 lb (500 g) fresh thin or regular Chinese egg noodles

peanut or corn oil for deep-frying

3 cloves garlic, finely chopped

3 cups (24 fl oz/750 ml) canned coconut milk (2 x 12-fl oz/375-ml cans), unshaken

2 tablespoons red curry paste, or to taste

1½ teaspoons curry powder

½ teaspoon ground turmeric

12 oz (375 g) chopped chicken meat

4 cups (1 qt/1 liter) chicken stock

3 tablespoons Thai fish sauce

1 teaspoon palm sugar or brown sugar

¼ cup (¾ oz/20 g) shredded green cabbage

juice of 1 lemon

GARNISHES

2 tablespoons fried shallot flakes (see page 149)

chopped cilantro (fresh coriander)

2 green (spring) onions, thinly sliced

1 lemon, cut into 6 wedges

✧ Bring a large pot three-fourths full of water to a boil. Gently pull the strands of noodles apart, then drop them into the boiling water. Return to a boil and cook for 1 minute. Pour into a colander and rinse with cold running water. Drain well, shaking off excess water.

✧ Using paper towels, pat dry 1 cup (6 oz/185 g) of the cooked noodles. Pour oil to a depth of 2 inches (5 cm) into a small saucepan and heat to 375°F (190°C). Add the noodles. Using a pair of long chopsticks or tongs, stir gently to separate the strands and fry until golden brown, about 30 seconds. Lift out the noodles and place on paper towels to drain. Remove the pan from the heat. Crumble the noodles into small chunks.

✧ Place 2 tablespoons of the oil used to fry the noodles in a large saucepan over medium heat. Add the garlic and sauté until browned, about 1 minute. There should be a thick layer of cream on top of each unshaken can of coconut milk. Spoon off ½ cup (4 fl oz/125 ml) of the cream from each can and add it to the saucepan. Increase heat to medium-high and cook, stirring frequently, to a gentle boil. Add the red curry paste, curry powder, and turmeric and stir until smooth. Reduce heat to medium and simmer until the mixture is thick and the oil begins to separate around the edges and rise to the surface, about 5 minutes.

✧ Add the chicken and cook until cooked through, about 2 minutes. Increase heat to high. Add remaining coconut milk, the stock, fish sauce, sugar, and cabbage and stir well. Gently boil for a further 8 minutes.

✧ Divide the boiled noodles among 6 warmed bowls. Stir the lemon juice into the soup and ladle equal amounts over the noodles. Garnish with the crumbled fried noodles, fried shallots, cilantro, and green onions. Place a lemon wedge on top of each serving and serve hot.

chicken soup
with potato patties

serves 6

CHICKEN STOCK

1 chicken, 2¹/₂ lb
(1.25 kg), cut into 6 pieces

3 leafy celery tops

1 yellow onion, quartered

2 cinnamon sticks

2 cardamom pods

SPICE PASTE

3 lemongrass stalks,
tender heart section only,
coarsely chopped

4 fresh galangal slices,
1 inch (2.5 cm) in diameter,
(or 2 dried slices, soaked
in water for 30 minutes,
drained, and chopped)

1 yellow onion, coarsely
chopped

4 cloves garlic, peeled

6 candlenuts or blanched
almonds

1 piece fresh ginger,
1¹/₂ inches (4 cm) long,
peeled and chopped

2 tablespoons ground
coriander

1 teaspoon black pepper

1 teaspoon turmeric

2 teaspoons sugar

1 teaspoon salt

about 3 tablespoons water

2 tablespoons peanut or
corn oil

POTATO PATTIES

1 lb (500 g) baking
potatoes, peeled and
boiled until tender

1 green (spring) onion,
finely chopped

¹/₂ teaspoon salt

1 egg, lightly beaten

vegetable oil for frying

For the stock, place the chicken in a large saucepan and add water to cover. Bring to a boil over high heat, skimming off any scum. Add the celery tops, onion, cinnamon, and cardamom. Reduce heat to low. Cover partially and simmer until the chicken is cooked through, about 40 minutes. Transfer the chicken breasts to a plate and let cool. Simmer stock 20–30 minutes further. Let the stock cool, then strain through a sieve into a bowl. Let stand until the fat rises to the surface. Using a large spoon, skim off fat and discard. This makes about 8 cups (2 qt/2 l).

Skin and bone the chicken breasts and hand shred the meat with the grain. Reserve the remaining chicken pieces for another use.

For the spice paste, using a blender, blend the lemongrass, galangal, onion, garlic, candlenuts or almonds, ginger, coriander, pepper, turmeric, sugar, and salt. Add water as needed to blend to a smooth paste.

In a large saucepan over medium heat, warm the oil. Stir in the spice paste and cook, stirring, until fragrant, about 5 minutes. Add the stock and simmer for 15 minutes. Keep warm.

For the patties, in a large bowl, combine the potatoes, green onion, salt, and egg. Using a potato masher or fork, mash the mixture thoroughly. Form twelve 1-inch (2.5-cm) balls and flatten each into a patty 1½ inches (4 cm) in diameter.

In a deep-frying pan, pour oil to 1 inch (2.5 cm). Heat to 375°F (190°C). Fry patties, a few at a time, until golden brown on the underside, about 3 minutes. Turn and brown the other side, about 1 minute further. Transfer to paper towels to drain. Keep warm. Fry remaining patties.

To serve, bring the stock to a simmer. Distribute the shredded chicken evenly among six soup bowls and ladle the hot stock on top. Garnish each bowl with 2 potato patties. Serve hot.

glossary

anchovy paste

A flavoring made from ground anchovies, vinegar, spices, and water, anchovy paste is available in convenient tubes.

bamboo shoots

These are the shoots of a type of bamboo plant. They are cut when small and tender and can be bought in Asian supermarkets or in cans. Refrigerated in an airtight container, they will keep for a few days.

bean sprouts

These sprouts are germinated beans— mung bean sprouts are the most popular in Asian cooking. Store in an airtight container for up to several days.

bok choy

Some may know this as a type of Chinese cabbage—it has fleshy white stalks and is shaped somewhat like spinach. Napa cabbage is another variety. It can be used in the same way as spinach and cabbage.

cayenne pepper

This is a hot, pungent powder made from several types of chiles. Stored in an airtight container, it will keep in a cool, dry place for several months.

chiles

Sometimes called hot peppers, there are hundreds of varieties of chiles—they are sold fresh, pickled, dried, ground, minced, and flaked. Over 100 varieties are from Mexico, including jalapeño, a large, hot chile (a chipotle is a dried, smoked jalapeño). The ancho chile is a mild, sweet, pungent dried chile. Chile oil is simply vegetable oil in which red chiles have been steeped. It is commonly used in Chinese cooking. Chiles contain oils that burn eyes and skin, so always wear rubber gloves to protect your hands when handling them.

coriander

Cilantro (fresh coriander) is related to parsley (it is sometimes called Chinese parsley) and is used widely to flavor Asian dishes, as well as Indian and Mexican food. Store it in a glass of water, much as you would cut flowers, and cover it loosely with a plastic bag. Refrigerate for up to a week, changing the water each day. Dried coriander seeds are used in many European and Asian recipes and in curry powders.

cumin

This ancient aromatic spice is available in both powder and seed form and is widely used in Middle Eastern, Mediterranean, and Asian cooking. It is a key ingredient in curry powder and some chile powders.

fish sauce

This pungent, bottled sauce is used in Southeast Asia in much the same way as soy sauce. It is very strong and salty (unsalted versions are also available) and there are many varieties, including Thai and Vietnamese, most of them interchangeable. It keeps indefinitely in the refrigerator.

five-spice powder

Widely used in Chinese cooking, this is a pungent mixture of cinnamon, cloves, fennel, star anise, and Sichuan pepper.

galangal

This rhizome is used widely in Asian cooking in a similar way to ginger, which it resembles in appearance and flavor. Fresh galangal can be difficult to find outside of Asia, but dried galangal is often stocked in Asian markets. Fresh ginger can be substituted if galangal is not available.

groundnut (peanut) oil

This oil is made from pressing peanuts. It has a high smoke point and so is very popular for frying. Chinese groundnut oil has a distinctive peanut flavor that other varieties lack. If stored in a dark, cool place, it will keep indefinitely.

hoisin sauce

This mixture of soybeans, garlic, chiles, and spices is usually used as a condiment. Bottled hoisin sauce will keep indefinitely if refrigerated once opened.

hot bean paste

Made from a fermented soybean sauce (miso) and crushed hot chiles, this Asian condiment sharpens the flavors of and thickens all kinds of foods. Look for it in jars or cans in Asian supermarkets. It stays fresh indefinitely if refrigerated.

mushrooms

There are many varieties of mushrooms available, both fresh and dried. The most common mushroom is dome-shaped, with a white, cream, or brown cap, short stalk, and mild flavor. Oyster mushrooms are fan shaped and can be wild or cultivated. Shiitakes are floppy and meaty with dark brown caps (the stems are usually discarded). Straw mushrooms are tiny and range from very pale when young to almost black when mature. They can be difficult to find fresh, but are often available canned. Always store mushrooms in brown paper bags, never in plastic, which makes them slimy.

oyster sauce

A combination of oysters, soy sauce, salt, and water, this sauce is popular in Asian cooking, particularly in stir-fries. It comes in bottles and should be refrigerated after opening to avoid mold.

rice wine

A wine fermented from rice, this is usually low in alcohol. The most famous rice wines are probably the Japanese sake and *mirin*. There are many varieties of Chinese rice wine available in Asian supermarkets.

sage

Gray-green sage has a slightly bitter taste and a distinctive aroma. It often partners poultry and is one of the major seasonings used to flavor sausages.

salsa

"Salsa" is Spanish for "sauce." The term refers to a Mexican condiment and dipping sauce, similar to ketchup, which is normally red and is made with tomatoes, chiles, onion, and spices. Green salsa is also available—it is usually a combination of tomatillos, green chiles, and cilantro (fresh coriander). Once opened, salsas can be stored in the refrigerator for 4–5 days.

sesame oil

Sesame seed is used in savory and sweet dishes alike. Sesame oil tastes of the seed from which it is produced and is used mainly as a seasoning for its nutty flavor.

Sichuan peppers

This mildly hot spice is a native of China. It is a berry from a prickly ash tree and, although similar to pepper, is not related to it. Sichuan pepper is one of the main ingredients of five-spice powder and of many dishes from China's Sichuan province.

soy sauce

Soy sauce is one the most popular and best understood of all Asian ingredients. For many, it is synonymous with Asian cooking. It is made from fermented soy beans, with the addition of wheat or barley. There are many varieties available but, generally speaking, they range from light to dark. Light soy sauce is thin and saltier than dark soy, and it doesn't spoil the color of food. Dark soy sauce is thicker, darker, and less salty. With the addition of sugar and malt sugar, it becomes sweet soy sauce.

sweet chile sauce

This ketchup-like sauce made with sugar, tomatoes, bell peppers (capsicums), vinegar, and spices is usually used as a condiment or dipping sauce, but is sometimes added to recipes for extra sweetness and bite.

tamarind

Also known as the Indian date, this is the fruit of a tree grown in Africa, Asia, and India. It produces pods (similar to a broad bean), that are sun dried and then mixed with salt to form a smooth, dark brown, soft block. It can be also refined further to form a thick sauce, known as tamarind concentrate. Tamarind's unique, sweet-tart flavor is often used to give a sharp, tangy edge to curries, braises, and sauces.

tomatillos

Despite the name, tomatillos are not tomatoes or their relatives; they are small green ground cherries. Their tart, lemony flavor adds bite to many Mexican sauces and stews. They are available fresh at some gourmet food markets and in cans at well-stocked supermarkets.

index

Page numbers in italics refer to photographs.

a note on measurements

U.S. cup measurements are used throughout this book. Slight adjustments may need to be made to quantities if Imperial or metric measures are used.

acknowledgments

Weldon Owen wishes to thank the following people for their help in producing this book: Nancy Sibtain (indexing); Angela Handley (proofreading); Kylie Mulquin (cover styling); Janine Flew (cover food preparation); Lena Lowe, Lynn Humphries (cover props); Ad-Libitum/ Stuart Bowey (cover photo).

sandwich
salad barb
noodlesdu
kabobstam
marinated
spaghettin